Cooking Your Way to Calm

Cooking Your Way to Calm

Julie Ohana, LMSW

sheldon PRESS

First published by Sheldon Press in 2025
An imprint of John Murray Press

1

This book is for information or educational purposes only and is not
intended to act as a substitute for medical advice or treatment.
Any person with a condition requiring medical attention should
consult a qualified medical practitioner or suitable therapist.

A CIP catalogue record for this title is available from the British Library

Library of Congress Control Number: 2025934248

Trade Paperback ISBN 978 1 399 82266 4
ebook ISBN 978 1 399 82267 1

Typeset by KnowledgeWorks Global Ltd.

Printed and bound in the United States of America

John Murray Press policy is to use papers that are natural, renewable and
recyclable products and made from wood grown in sustainable forests.
The logging and manufacturing processes are expected to conform to the
environmental regulations of the country of origin.

John Murray Press
Carmelite House
50 Victoria Embankment
London EC4Y 0DZ

www.sheldonpress.co.uk

John Murray Press, part of Hodder & Stoughton Limited
An Hachette UK company

The authorised representative in the EEA is Hachette Ireland, 8 Castlecourt Centre,
Dublin 15, D15 XTP3, Ireland (email: info@hbgi.ie)

To Papa and Grandma who always made me feel deeply loved and nourished me in every possible way. You inspired me to care for others in a multitude of ways, most importantly around the dinner table with amazing food and wonderful people.

Contents

About the Author

Julie's journey with culinary art therapy began 25 years ago while attending Yeshiva University's Wurzweiler School of Social Work in New York City. While working to earn a Master of Social Work, Julie wrote a thesis on the therapeutic benefits of cooking. She knew very early on in her career that cooking had the ability to help make people happier.

While continuing on her social work path, Julie spent time working in Chicago at an inpatient substance abuse treatment facility. Julie worked with women who struggled with addiction as well as other mental health disorders. Julie was inspired watching the women come together around mealtime and help to prepare their own dinners.

Julie went on to spend the next decade of her career working with teenagers in a private Jewish high school in her hometown of West Bloomfield, Michigan. Julie worked as the school social worker, helping students and their parents navigate the tumultuous times of their teenage years. Once again, she utilized the power of cooking whenever she had the opportunity to integrate this practice.

During the last number of years, Julie has maintained a private practice utilizing talk therapy and culinary art therapy. Julie works with individuals, families, couples, and larger groups to help them explore the benefits of this practice. In 2019, Julie self-published a culinary art therapy (CAT) curriculum to help other mental health professionals incorporate CAT into their own practices.

Julie has been interviewed by countless magazines and news outlets. She has spoken at several major American universities, including Michigan State University, and been featured in media outlets all over the world including *The New York Times*, *The Huffington Post*, *Good Housekeeping*, *Women's Health Magazine*, *CNN*, *The Washington Post*, and on the TV show *The Doctors*.

In addition to the passion Julie has for sharing CAT with the world, she is equally as passionate about her own beautiful family. Julie has been married for 16 years to a wonderful man who shares her love of cooking, food, and family. The couple have two incredible teenage children, a daughter who enjoys chopping cabbage salad and decorates the most beautiful cakes and a son who is a master shakshuka maker and has a knack for finding fantastic online recipes for the family to try together.

Prologue

I have been cooking, brainstorming, and patiently waiting for the day to arrive when I could share my passion with you. I wrote this book because I care so deeply and believe so strongly in the benefit of cooking as a way to heal from anxiety and all the wounds that it creates.

I feel eternally grateful to have been raised in a home where I felt unwavering love and attention. My needs were always tended to, and my soul was nourished along with my belly. I grew up knowing the deep impact that love that originated in the kitchen had on me and could have on so many others. There is great power that comes from feeding someone. When nourishing yourself and the people you love, the benefits are so much greater than just a tasty meal.

My journey with culinary art therapy began 25 years ago while attending Yeshiva University's Wurzweiler School of Social Work in New York City. While working to earn a master's in social work, I wrote a thesis on the therapeutic benefits of cooking because I knew very early on in my career that cooking had the ability to help make people happier.

A few years ago, I began concentrating on culinary art therapy. My private practice utilizes talk therapy as well as culinary art therapy, and I work with individuals, families, couples, and larger groups to help them explore the benefits of this practice.

As you read along, cook, reflect, and learn, you will find tips and tools along the way that will help you to make changes in your life that will allow you to feel lighter and happier and live the life that you want to live. The features in this book will not only help you learn more about yourself but enable you to have a deep sense of understanding that will allow you to make power-ful choices about how you live your life.

Among this book's featured sections are:

- Making the Connection
- Before You Begin, Consider This

- Name Three...
- Goal Setting
- Recipes
- Reflections.

Please use this book in a way that will help put your mind and body at ease. My hope is that every reader has a village filled with supportive people to help make life better. But I also know that, some days, it is hard to call on that village, and it is crucial that every person feels empowered to have their very own toolbox to pull out and make use of. I hope this book feels like that toolbox.

My most sincere hope for you is that this book will become your trusted guide as you look to make your life better. I hope it fills you with hope and knowledge and with many, many delicious dishes along the way.

Foreword

Food has always been at the center of my world. As a self-proclaimed foodie, I have always been a proud member of the clean plate club. Many of my most cherished childhood memories revolve around food. I can still smell my mom's matzoh ball soup cooking while I helped her set the table for Rosh Hashanah. Summer trips to the pool were my favorite, I would swim for hours, get hot under the Michigan sun, and then happily end every swimming session with a hot order of crispy french fries from the snack grill. I only agreed to play in the snow with my little brother because after my mom would reward me with hot chocolate covered in mini marshmallows. I watched Food Network for hours on end, devouring every bit of culinary knowledge I could.

Julie, funnily enough, was my high school's social worker. I will never forget the time I skipped class to cry in her office. I was having boy problems, and she encouraged me to be confident, and stand up for myself. I genuinely owe her everything—because those "silly" boy problems I was dealing with in high school, weren't so silly after all. That boy? He's now my husband.

As you read, learn, and cook your way to calm—I promise you're in the best hands.

This cookbook will help you recognize the value in spending time in the kitchen. Whenever I have a stressful day at work or I'm feeling anxious, making dinner at the end of a long day is my time to unwind, relax, slow down, and reconnect with myself and my family. As soon as I begin, my two-year-old son scoots his toddler tower up to the counter to watch what "Mama" is doing.

As Julie so importantly emphasizes, cooking is an incredible way to express your inner creativity. Personally, I don't measure anything when I cook. Just like a dancer improvising a routine, I freestyle my way through every meal I make. With practice, you too, will learn that cooking can be one of the most calming and creatively fulfilling experiences in your day—and with Julie as your guide, you will become a master.

There's something beautifully and incredibly grounding about using your hands to create something nourishing. Cooking offers us an opportunity to be fully present—a sensory experience that quiets the noise in our minds and brings us back to the here and now. In a world that constantly demands our attention, the simple act of slicing a vegetable or stirring a pot can feel like meditation. I try to put my phone in the other room while or cook or turn it off, as it's a sacred time for me. This is the gift Julie gives us with this book: the reminder that healing doesn't always require grand gestures. Sometimes, it starts with a cutting board and a knife.

The kitchen isn't *just* a kitchen. It's a safe space—a place of refuge where you can share your innermost thoughts and feelings, solve problems, and deepen your relationships with the people you love, including yourself.

With love,

Danielle Brown

Founder of HealthyGirl Kitchen and two-time *The New York Times* bestselling author

Part 1
Get Out of Your Own Way

Chapter 1

Culinary Art Therapy—Yes, It's a Real Thing

Hello! Thanks so much for welcoming me into your home, your heart, and your kitchen.

If you picked this book up from the shelf among the countless books about anxiety and depression, my guess is you are here for one of two reasons. Either you are someone who already finds joy and solace in the kitchen, mixing and chopping your way to a state of calm and peace, or you are someone who has struggled with anxiety and has yet to find the right tool to help you manage the burdens of these symptoms.

Either way, you have picked up the right book. So many people are consumed each and every day with stress and the daily struggles of life. Every day they may ask themselves:

- How do I balance career and family?
- How do I care for myself, make time for friends, and still prioritize my health and well-being?
- How do I accomplish all the daily tasks without feeling like I am drowning or a nervous wreck?

If this resonates with you, there is a reason for it. Anxiety disorders are the most common mental health concern in the United States, where over 40 million adults (19.1 percent according to the National Institute of Mental Health) are diagnosed with one. There are likely millions more struggling with undiagnosed anxiety.

I have been working with clients for over 20 years, and the most common struggles I see in my practice are depression and anxiety, which often go hand in hand.

There are many tools to help people manage their symptoms; medication and talk therapy are two of them. While these help many people with their symptoms, sadly, for some, they are not always effective. This leaves some people struggling and feeling desperate to find a magic wand to make everything better. We know that no two people are exactly alike, however, and there is no one-size-fits-all solution: some tools work well for some people and some of those same tools do not help others at all. One commonality that all people do share, though, is that they all need to eat. They need to take care of themselves, and this always involves food. So if we know that everyone needs to feed themselves, why not get more out of the process than just a full belly?

Remember, I am not here to judge you, your anxious ways, or your cooking abilities. I am here to meet you right where you are and share my effective, compassionate approach for cooking your way to lower anxiety levels, more confidence, and your happiest life.

Becoming a Kitchen Coach

My culinary art therapy adventure began while I was a graduate student doing research for my thesis on how cooking can be a worthwhile therapeutic intervention.

Working as a therapist has been extremely rewarding. Connecting with people, supporting them in their hardest days, and celebrating their successes are things that I am beyond grateful to be present for. Early on in my practice, I provided talk therapy. I would use different cognitive behavioral therapy (CBT) techniques—a common type of therapy that aims to help people identify and change the negative thoughts and thought patterns influencing their behavior and mood. I utilized these tools with the same clients on my sofa for several months, often discussing the same issues, sometimes without much ability to implement change. I used to find myself coming home to my own kitchen after those sessions, eager to start chopping, mixing, and simmering delicious, filling ingredients to nourish myself and my family. I just knew I had to keep working to combine these two passions: helping people and cooking.

Some clients needed someone else to talk, support, and listen to them while other clients needed someone to join them on the journey and take action *with* them. This latter group needs a guide to get them truly activated, which means progressing from the *talking* phase and into the *action* phase. Using cooking, and being by my client's side to ask thought-provoking questions and make observations about their choices while they are cooking, lets them see for themselves the benefit of that action. Through our guided discussions, including questions to prompt reflection and directions with a clear focus and purpose, cooking allows for a moment of reprieve from anxiety and other negative emotions.

My role in this type of therapy serves as motivation and coach to the client. Just as some people find it easier to complete a workout in the gym if they have a personal trainer by their side, I am that mental health trainer in the kitchen. My most fulfilling professional days are seeing how this practice helps someone instantly. Not only is it possible for some to experience immediate relief, but the skills learned can be applied over and over again to help the client ease any returning negative emotions.

My caseload has grown over the years. My individual clients grew into small groups and families, and with the move to online therapy (hello, pandemic silver lining) I am now reaching people all over the globe. I am seeing and watching my clients take deeper, easier breaths, laugh through some tears, and realize there is a simple task that can help them focus on something other than racing thoughts. Concluding a session with a finished product that can be consumed and enjoyed provides an incredible feeling of satisfaction and confidence for both me and my clients. The benefits that come from skills learned in the kitchen are life altering.

An Appetizer to Understand Better

Let me tell you a bit about Chris. Chris reached out to me about a year ago looking for support. She lived with her husband, had a son in college, and worked part time for her husband's company. In her free time, she enjoyed gardening and running. She worked hard to take care of herself and look after her family. Chris had sought out therapy in the past when she had felt anxious and had emotional lows. She generally ate well, stayed active, and made healthy life choices, but recently she had been feeling down, worried, and just not "herself." She contacted me because, even though she was not an active home cook, she did enjoy hosting and bringing people together. Chris thought culinary art therapy might be beneficial for her, and she was right!

Through our weekly sessions, Chris was able to identify areas of stress and worry for herself. Through conversations about following recipes and decision making, she realized just how much she lacked confidence. That lack of confidence was causing her to worry about her professional role and her ability to make positive choices, and it was having a negative impact not only on the company and her professional life but also on her marriage.

Through problem solving while cooking, Chris was able to gain more confidence in her abilities in the kitchen and learn how to apply that same confidence outside the kitchen. When she was missing some key recipe ingredients and was guided through the process of finding substitutions or omitting ingredients, she saw that she could make those decisions without the recipe failing. When she applied that same degree of patience, awareness, and communication outside the kitchen, she noticed that she was better able to handle the curve balls that came her way each day. She felt more empowered and less anxious and depressed.

She got out of her own way!

Behavioral Activation: Why Cooking Works

Since my initial research all the way back in graduate school, and over my twenty-plus years as a licensed clinical social worker, I have continued to learn more about anxiety and its impact on my clients. Because anxiety impacts the lives of so many millions of people worldwide, it is essential for us to understand where this anxiety comes from, how it impacts our daily lives, and what we can do to decrease these struggles.

Over the course of my career, I've seen the transformative power of cooking to reduce stress, enhance relationships, boost confidence, and help my clients feel happier overall. If you've ever pulled a fragrant tray of fudgy brownies out of the oven, you've experienced a twinge of why cooking is so effective at lowering stress and anxiety.

This is all due to behavioral activation. A tool of cognitive behavioral therapy, behavioral activation means engaging in an activity that you find personally rewarding or that gives you a sense of accomplishment, according to Jacqueline Gollan, PhD, an associate professor of psychiatry and behavioral sciences at Northwestern University, Illinois. She adds that even seeing the pleasure of someone else eating pumpkin bread with chocolate chips that you made for them can improve your sense of well-being.

Research from the University of Michigan tells us that anxiety and depression come from parts of our brain that are trying to protect us by getting us to avoid anxiety inducing circumstances or isolate ourselves. This means that as long as we are following the lead of the anxiety and depression, we will continue to feel less motivated and want to avoid and isolate.

Instead, by stimulating changes to our brain through rewarding activities, we can make ourselves feel better right away. An example that most people are familiar with is exercise. Physical movement produces endorphins in the brain that lift mood while they are in the bloodstream. This is why so often you hear people telling us to go for a walk or a run to feel better. Cooking works in much the same way. Not only is cooking a physical activity that can get endorphins going, it also breaks the avoid-and-isolate cycle in the brain.

Once you begin the process of cooking, behavioral activation has begun. And the best part? The mood-boosting process concludes with a warm chocolate cake or a tasty chicken dinner. Can you relate to the satisfying feelings that come with serving your family or loved ones a delicious dessert or meal? This sense of accomplishment is exactly what can lead to lower anxiety. And the good news is, we have a wealth of opportunities each and every day to try out behavioral activation to lessen anxiety. Cooking is an opportunity to nurture our loved ones with our meals, and at the same time, we can be practicing self-care. In short, behavioral activation is the reason why cooking is such an effective therapy.

In Part 2, you will experience how the eight-week plan covered in this book will help you develop multiple important life skills that will lower stress, worry, and anxiety. The following are the skills that will be utilized (and the chapters that focus on them):

Mindfulness (Chapter 4): Mindfulness—a mental state of focused attention on the present moment and acceptance of our feelings, thoughts, and physical sensations—is a powerful way to lower anxiety. Meditation is a common way to practice mindfulness, but if you are like me and have a hard time sitting still for more than five minutes without getting restless, you may need an alternative plan to practice mindfulness. For some, an ideal way to practice being in the moment is by sitting legs crossed and fingers pinched; for others, it may be following the step-by-step direction of a recipe and completing small tasks one at a time.

Patience (Chapter 4): Anxiety and patience are like the proverbial chicken and egg: We don't know which comes first but we do know that both trigger stress and an overactive brain and can cause insomnia, fatigue, trouble concentrating, lack of motivation, and, of course, unhappiness. Learning to practice patience is a skill that helps keep anxiety at bay. Cooking offers many opportunities to practice being patient: Can you smell the simmering chicken soup that boils away for hours? When was the last time you spent 20 minutes mincing red pepper for gazpacho?

Communication (Chapter 5): Think about a time when you tried to explain something of importance to a friend or coworker and they were not understanding your message. Think about how frustrated this made you feel. Perhaps you could even feel your blood pressure rising. That frustration can lead to anxiety. It also works the other way around, with common anxiety symptoms such as racing thoughts and unorganized speech leading to poor communication. Both scenarios only enhance mood-related struggles. It is a vicious cycle that can be broken in the kitchen. There are many ways to practice communication around food. Cooking with a partner is one way, but simply writing a note to go along with a delivery of cookies encourages open and clear lines of communication, a skill that can be taken out of the kitchen and into the workplace or the home to lessen anxiety.

Problem solving (Chapter 6): Since 1982, therapists have been practicing solution-focused brief therapy (SFBT) with clients struggling with anxiety. A core belief of this approach is: "Small steps can lead to big changes." Helping someone manage anxiety is often rooted in helping them solve small dilemmas or situations. What can you do when you are baking muffins and you run out of sugar? Could you use honey? Could you use other natural sweeteners? Every recipe offers an opportunity to find solutions to safe, nonconsequential problems. The more proficient you become at solving cooking problems, the easier it becomes to find solutions to larger problems.

Stress and time management (Chapter 7): Oftentimes, stress and anxiety manifest themselves with several of the same symptoms — uneasiness, tension headaches, high blood pressure, and loss of sleep, to name a few. The main difference between them is that stress is a response to something external like a fight with a friend or an upcoming exam or deadline. Stress typically exists for a finite period of time. Anxiety is often the way that a person responds to or copes with stress, an internal response. Prolonged stress levels can easily lead to anxiety if the symptoms are not identified. Spending time cooking in the kitchen is a great way to identify stressors and the way in which you respond and manage the stress. How do you manage to juggle multiple recipes while making a meal? How do you organize your ingredients and time to have everything ready in a specific amount of time? When you have the ability to practice identifying and using coping strategies, you become more able to manage stress reactions outside of the kitchen.

Relationships (Chapter 8): Dr. Helen Riess, director of the Empathy and Relational Science Program at Massachusetts General Hospital, Boston, and author of *The Empathy Effect*, explains how feelings of loneliness can stimulate anxiety, not to mention increase inflammation, which in turn activates pain centers and triggers other neurological responses in the brain. What better way to keep loneliness at bay than by connecting with a friend or loved one? No matter whether they are physically present in the space with you or a recipe conjures the memory of a loved one. As writer Laurie Colwin so eloquently said: "No one who cooks, cooks alone. Even at her most solitary, a cook in the kitchen is surrounded by generations of cooks past, the advice and menus of cooks present, and the wisdom of cookbook writers."

Self-esteem (Chapter 9): Living with low self-esteem can harm your mental health and lead to depression and anxiety. Low self-esteem also exacerbates doubts and fears, which can lead to further avoidance of healthy behavior. Cooking provides low-risk, realistic ways to increase self-esteem and boost confidence. Seeing a positive reaction from others when delivering homemade treats or taking that first delicious solo bite when you succeed at a new recipe creates an immediate boost in self-esteem.

Getting out of your own way and into the kitchen will...

- help you to realize the connection between anxiety and the skills that will keep it at bay
- teach you practical, useful tasks to lower anxiety in the moment
- offer you a way to enhance your real-world skills, making you a happier, healthier person
- provide you with step-by-step directions through simple and delicious recipes that you will want to cook time and time again
- show you ways to connect to loved ones that will bring joy and confidence to your life
- prompt reflection and self-discovery through the practice of the skills.

An Anxious Apple

Before you can do anything to lessen your anxiety, it is crucial that you understand exactly what it is and the important difference between *stress* and *anxiety*. We all experience stress (external events or aspects in our lives that are temporary) but we all cope with these events differently. Some of us can manage these events without experiencing a racing heart, or sleepless nights, or uncontrolled worry (i.e. anxiety). Learning more about how you experience anxiety, and, more importantly, how to best cope with and manage it, is the goal of the next eight weeks.

You may be asking yourself why you feel like you get more anxious than your partner or friends. Well, there are many reasons for that. Anxiety is complex and there are many contributing factors that determine who suffers from anxiety and who may not.

Some of these determining factors are:

- social/environmental
- socioeconomic
- psychological/biological.

Social and environmental factors include any negative life events that you may have experienced: Maybe your parents got divorced when you were young; maybe you were bullied in school; or maybe you experienced other childhood trauma. People who have suffered abuse, severe losses, or other adverse experiences are more likely to develop anxiety disorders. Socioeconomic factors include financial problems, housing problems, long working hours, and being unemployed for extended periods of time. Psychological and biological factors include physical or mental health problems. Sometimes, other health problems cause anxiety or might make it worse. Our genes also play a role in anxiety. If you have a relative that suffers with anxiety, then you are more likely to have the same struggle.

It is also important to remember that sometimes we have a hard time putting our thumb on the exact reason why we struggle, but, as frustrating as that can be, what really matters is what we decide to do to change it. You are here, and you made the decision to get out of your own way and get into your kitchen!

How do I know if I am nervous or anxious?

You may be experiencing any one or many of the following symptoms. Some people feel all these symptoms, and some people fluctuate between them at different points in their lives.

Physical symptoms	Emotional symptoms	Behavioral symptoms
fast or irregular heartbeat	irritability	teeth grinding
sweating	restlessness	changes in sex drive
trembling	feeling nervous	panic attacks
nausea	feeling on edge	social withdrawal
abdominal distress	trouble concentrating	compulsive behaviors
muscle tension	sense of impending danger	
headaches	panic	
backache	uncontrolled worry	
aches and pains		

Test Time

This diagnostic tool will help you become more aware of your unique ways of experiencing anxiety and help you to identify your level of anxiety. This check-in will serve as your baseline and help you monitor your feelings and symptoms as you experience and track your progress through the eight-week program in Part 2. Your responses should be based on your general experiences over the last few weeks.

Select the response that best describes the extent to which you experience each symptom.

0 = Not at all 1 = Mild 2 = Moderate 3 = Severe 4 = Very severe

Anxious mood

Worried, waiting for something bad, fearful anticipation, dread

0   1   2   3   4

Tension

Startle easily, restless, unable to relax

0   1   2   3   4

Insomnia

Hard time falling asleep and/or staying asleep, general fatigue, nightmares, lack of motivation

0   1   2   3   4

Depressed mood

Loss of interest, lack of pleasure, sadness, irritability

0   1   2   3   4

Pain

Aches, stiffness, grinding or clenching of the teeth, headaches

0   1   2   3   4

Panic

Palpitations, chest pain or tightness, fainting feeling, hard to breathe

0   1   2   3   4

Fears

Afraid of darkness, strangers, being left alone, being in crowds

0   1   2   3   4

Scoring: Count up the total number of points.

Score total: _____

A total less than 7 means mild anxiety symptoms, 8–12 is mild to moderate, 13–15 is moderate to severe. 16 and above is very severe.

Reflection

Food for thought

Q: How does it feel to embark on this experience?

A: ....

....

....

....

....

....

....

Q: what have you learned about anxiety so far?

A: ....

....

....

....

....

....

....

Q: Was your baseline anxiety score surprising to you? Was it lower or higher than you expected it would be?

A: ....

....

....

....

....

....

Q: What questions have you got? How can you answer them?

A: ....

....

....

....

....

....

Notes

Chapter 2

Get Your Mind and Your Pantry Prepped

Now that you have a deeper understanding of what anxiety is and how you yourself experience anxiety, what culinary art therapy is, and how this book will help you, it's time to set you up for success. This means taking some time to prepare mentally, and yes, your pantry needs some prepping, too.

This chapter will help get you into the right mindset for this adventure by offering best practices for mapping out this eight-week experience, including how to find and carve out times that you can complete each lesson. I'll also help you identify your support system, recognizing any people in your life that can either participate in the process when called upon or provide any other encouragement that you may find helpful. We will also set clear, measurable goals. It is important to set a goal for yourself before beginning so that you can measure your sense of accomplishment.

Setting the Stage (or the Table)

Typically, a great meal starts with some kind of plan. It takes list making, grocery shopping, time, and energy. Before this great meal can help you to feel less anxious, we need to "set the table," so to speak. That means clearing your mind and starting from a baseline point of calm.

Let's begin with an exercise that some refer to as the *333 rule*. The simplicity of the 333 rule brings immediate calm and focus. It can redirect you away from overwhelming feelings and thoughts so you can center yourself in the present moment. This immediate grounding can provide relief from anxiety attacks and help you regain control over your emotions and thoughts. I suggest you begin each week's assignment with this exercise, as well as any other time you feel overwhelmed or are having a hard time focusing on the task at hand. You can use this in the kitchen as well as outside the kitchen when you are at work, out with friends, or simply feeling a sense of panic creep up and you are in need of tools to help keep those feelings at bay.

I'm going to ask you to identify three different items that are related to your cooking experience as well as your senses. By focusing on the specific answers with something visual, you will be able to focus on something different that will help diminish anxious thoughts and make room for helpful, positive, or even neutral thoughts.

Let's begin: As you answer each question, picture the item in your mind's eye. Try to imagine as much detail as possible. Think of the color, size, shape, and even smell of the item. The more detail you can conjure in your mind, the more room you create for the item and the less room there will be for the anxiety.

Now, take a deep breath and answer in your head or in writing as you exhale:

Name three kitchen utensils that you most often use:

1. ....

2. ....

3. ....

Name three flavors that you enjoyed in your last meal:

1. ....

2. ....

3. ....

Name three ingredients that are currently in your refrigerator:

1. ....

2. ....

3. ....

How do you feel? Did this exercise make you feel calmer? More focused? Are you feeling ready to move forward and begin cooking? This is the goal of the exercise. Remember, this is a tool that you can choose to use as often as you need to. Use it when you feel overwhelmed, confused, or start to feel your heart race. It's okay to take a time out and recenter yourself at any point that you feel is necessary or would be beneficial.

Timeline

Let's talk about the timeline for this experience. Everyone is different, and everyone has different lives filled with different responsibilities and flexibility. If you are someone juggling a demanding career, a busy family, and little sleep, don't push yourself and rush through this experience. Remember, this program is meant to lessen your stress, not increase it. I want you to feel empowered to plan and make decisions that feel best suited for your lifestyle.

If your life is already filled close to capacity, **dedicate one evening or one weekend afternoon a month** to give yourself some time to focus on each recipe. Be realistic with yourself and your commitments.

Setting aside a few hours each month is the maximum length of time to wait between sessions. You want to be able to remember each session as you go into a new session, because the lessons and experiences will build on each other and be cumulative. If you wait too long between cooking sessions, you may not be getting the most out of the experience.

On the opposite end of the spectrum, if you have an abundance of flexibility with time and responsibilities, **set aside time for a weekly session or maybe even two sessions a week**. If you are very eager to get started and work through the eight-week experience, keep in mind you should not rush through and race to the food finish line. This experience is asking you to allow time for reflection and processing. It is paramount that you really lean into that reflection opportunity because, at the end of the experience, you will end up with more lessons learned, a stronger sense of skills gained, and even more chances for understanding and growth.

As you embark on this journey, there will be moments of quiet reflection and tasks for you to complete on your own. That may require you to give thought and make plans for solo time in the kitchen or somewhere else where you can sit, uninterrupted, to think, reflect, and write your notes. Considering that the kitchen is the grand central hub of many homes, think about times when you will have the ability to use the space without getting in the way of a roommate, partner, or kids. You want to make sure others won't be distracting you or getting in your way as well.

Another aspect to consider as you schedule your time to cook is the recipe you will be making. If the dish can be enjoyed at a mealtime, make plans to use the kitchen and enjoy the food for your meal. There is certainly nothing wrong with accomplishing multiple goals with one task. If the dish is not for a meal, you have the opportunity to be more flexible with your time.

Support System

Roommates, spouses, partners, kids, these are all people who have potential to be part of your support system. Consider the ways in which people you share a physical space with can help you in this process.

There may be times when a session calls for a sous chef—your second-in-command in the kitchen and an extra pair of hands. Can you think of asking one of these people? There may be other times when you simply want a taste tester. Who is the right person for that job? In other sessions, you may be cooking a whole meal and dining with someone else. Who is the best person to support your journey? If you know someone is a super-picky eater and may not be interested in the flavors you are working with, they may not help you to feel successful. If someone else that you can think of really enjoys a variety of flavors and your company, they may be a great fit.

Remember, you do not have to limit your support to people who live in your household. This is a great opportunity to reach out to a friend or neighbor, or even extend a virtual invitation to someone far away whom you'd like to welcome into your kitchen over FaceTime or Zoom. If the pandemic taught us anything, we learned the importance of thinking outside of the box. The kitchen is a great place that allows room for that. With technology at your side, don't think twice about using your phone or laptop to provide an opportunity for connection and support.

Since flexibility is so important and one of the skills that we will work on, start here by considering ways that you can be flexible with your loved ones. Even if you feel alone and isolated, there is room to reach out and expand your circle. For hundreds and hundreds of years, "breaking bread" has helped connect people and bring them together. Usually, people are excited by an invitation to be fed, to feel nurtured, and to be cared for. This is a chance for you to grow that circle for yourself. It can be a chance to welcome new people into your home or strengthen a deeper sense of connection with someone already in your home. You are providing an opportunity for others to feel helpful as well. Everyone likes to feel that they can be impactful and make a difference to someone else. By extending this invitation you are opening that door for others.

Consider using this checklist to begin brainstorming who can be part of your support system. Add the name of a person or persons whom you could ask to fulfill that role.

- Grocery shopper _____
- Taste tester _____
- Sous chef _____
- Dinner guest _____
- Dishwasher helper _____
- Listener/person to reflect with _____

Setting Goals

Sometimes the idea of goal setting can be overwhelming and seem more daunting than helpful. Stop for a moment and reframe the idea of a goal to a simple intention. Goals do not need to be giant, life-altering markers; they can simply just mean deciding what to be aware of and what you intend to do. Setting an intention for yourself as you embark on this journey will allow for the maximum benefit from this experience. It is crucial to the process that you have a level of awareness for what you are trying and hoping to achieve. These goals can be general goals for the experience or they can be more specific goals that are targeted toward each lesson. You will have an opportunity at the start of each session to consider what your goal is and how you will know if it has been achieved.

You may have purchased this book because you have a goal of feeling less nervous and less on edge. You may love to cook and feel your most comfortable in the kitchen, and are looking to expand on that time in an already familiar and calming place.

You may be a new cook, looking to gain more confidence and familiarity in the epicenter of your home while at the same time looking to build life skills that will enable you to lead a happier, more grounded lifestyle.

Consider the person you are striving to be at the end of this adventure. Who do you want to see in that reflection when you look in the mirror? How will you know you have achieved those goals?

My goal/intention for completing the eight-week culinary therapy experience is:

I will know I have achieved my goal when I feel:

....

....

....

....

Pantry Prep

Once you're mentally prepped, it's time to consider preparing your pantry. It's a good idea to have some basic staples we'll use frequently on hand in your pantry. Many of these, such as salt, pepper, peanut butter, and olive oil, may already be there! Keep in mind that cooking has the potential to be flexible. Flexibility when cooking provides a beautiful opportunity for us to practice a skill that is often required in life outside of the kitchen. You can always find a substitution if you're missing an ingredient. In fact, that is part of the challenge.

A well-stocked pantry is intended to help support you in this process, not to be an intimidating task that you feel pressure to keep up with. This list is to help guide you and to get you started with many of the tools and ingredients that will be included in this process. Of course, you will need to supplement your pantry with trips to the store for fresh ingredients and produce, but these pantry staples will provide a solid foundation for cooking many meals to come.

Pantry items to keep on hand...

Dry goods

Baking powder
Baking soda
Beans (black,
kidney, chickpeas)
BBQ sauce
Brown sugar
Canned tuna fish
Canned corn
Chocolate chips
Cocoa powder
Crackers

Crushed tomatoes
Flour
Honey
Maple syrup
Olive oil
Olives
Pasta
Peanut butter
Pickles
Pine nuts
Rice

Stock (veggie or
chicken)
Sugar
Tahini paste
Tomato paste
Tomato sauce
Vanilla
Vegetable oil
Vinegar (apple cider)

In the fridge

Broccoli
Butter
Cabbage
Cauliflower
Cheese
Cucumber

Eggs
Garlic
Heavy cream
Jams
Lettuce
Milk

Miso
Onions
Peppers
Shallots
Tomatoes
Yogurt (plain)

Spices and seeds

Bay leaves
Cinnamon
Crushed red
pepper flakes
Cumin
Dried dill

Dried parsley
Garlic powder
Onion powder
Panko breadcrumbs
Paprika (smoked and
sweet)

Pepper
Salt
Sesame seeds
Red pepper flakes
Turmeric
Za'atar

Condiments

Assorted mustards
Hot sauce

Mayonnaise

Worcestershire
sauce

Kitchen utensils to keep on hand...

Mixing bowls
Measuring cups
Measuring spoons
Mixing spoon
Spatula
Whisk

Baking pans
Glass baking dish
Food processor
Blender
Electric mixer
Immersion blender

Parchment paper
Aluminum foil
Medium stockpot
Large frying pan

Time to get into the kitchen...

Notes

Part 2
Get into the Kitchen

Chapter 3

Week One: The Power of Food and Memory

Making the Connection

Have you ever considered that the items in your childhood lunchbox were significant to your life later on? It sounds strange that an egg salad sandwich could represent something significant ten, twenty, or more years later, but in fact, it is possible. Many of our early memories revolve around food and that sandwich (or whatever food you think of as a young child) can remind us of moments that contribute to feelings or behaviors in our lives as adults today. Most therapists agree that childhood is the foundation for our sense of self and how we see ourselves later on in life.

The challenge is how to access that time in our lives and recall moments that are meaningful—both positive and challenging. Did you have a happy childhood? Were you anxious as a child? To learn more about ourselves, why we are the way we are, and why we make the choices we do, it is important to start at the beginning.

Many therapists successfully access this time in a person's life by asking simple questions about family background while a client is comfortably sitting on their sofa. They ask about your parents, siblings, school, and relevant history. For some people, these questions are a great way to unlock the door to childhood memories and explore the early years of life. For other people, however, that door remains locked and shut very tightly, making it impossible for anyone to access that period of time or those memories.

Culinary art therapy utilizes the senses to create a different kind of opportunity to access these memories using an edible key. A key to a secret back door, if you will.

Let me tell you a story about a bagel sandwich. Some people may not even agree that a bagel is a sandwich. (Have you ever debated whether a hot dog in a bun is considered a sandwich?) For the purpose of this work, we're going to accept that both a bagel and a hot dog are in fact a sandwich.

When I was a young girl, maybe five or six years old, I remember spending many Sunday brunches going to my paternal grandparents' house. We would stop and pick up a giant bag of assorted, freshly baked, warm bagels and all the toppings and spreads to go along with them. When we arrived at my grandparents' house, the potent and mildly offensive smell of sliced onions would greet me as soon as I stepped inside the door. I would try to forget about the onions and focus on the other items that I enjoyed, like the juicy tomatoes and the crisp leaves of green lettuce.

My bubbie (Yiddish for grandmother) had the table set and ready for us to all have a seat, come together, and build our own bagel sandwich for brunch. The grownups indulged in those stinky onions and other strange things like smoked fish and other salty toppings. I was always offered those bizarre additions, was even encouraged to try these unappealing items, but I declined and that was okay by them. I stuck to lettuce and tomato and cream cheese.

As I got older, the offer always stood, the encouragement remained, and my desire to try grew as well. Nowadays, when I build a bagel, I find myself reaching for smoked salmon. I enjoy the combination of lettuce, tomato, and salmon. I can taste the growth and the acceptance that it comes with. I still draw the line at the stinky onion, but I remain open to the possibility that maybe one day it will appeal to me.

The sense of smell and the related one of taste are the strongest of the senses that are tied to memory. Many have studied this phenomenon and refer to it as the "Proust effect" after the French novelist Marcel Proust. The significance of this wonder is not just about nostalgia, though. When we can unlock personal memories, we can better understand ourselves. This connection to our early self is beneficial because it gives us a different perspective on who we are and how we got here. We can then better understand our life experiences and choices. This will help provide the tools we need to create necessary or desired change in our lives.

~~~~~~~~~~~~~~~~~~~~

"Smell can instantly trigger an emotional response along with a memory, and our emotional states have a very strong effect on our physical well-being."

— Rachel Herz[1]

~~~~~~~~~~~~~~~~~~~~

As the Brown University neuroscientist Rachel Herz says, this emotional state has a strong effect on our physical well-being. If anxiety has roots in a specific time or situation, and you can actually remember that time and situation, instead of allowing the anxiety to dictate your well-being, you can actually do something about it. These memories can empower us and remind us that we do not need to just accept our lives as they are. You are the decision maker of your own life and you have the ability to take the reins when you choose to do so.

Before You Begin, Consider This

Now, let's grab those reins and take them on a stroll down memory lane, straight to your grade school cafeteria. We will explore memories that are evoked when you think of and create the dishes from that period in your life. What connections can we make about the person you are today and the person who existed all those years ago?

In Week 1 of our culinary art therapy journey, you will be making sandwiches because this is a common meal and lunch experience for many kids growing up going to school. Maybe, for some, sandwiches weren't a part of the childhood lunchbox. Feel free to be as creative and daring as you are inspired to be. This initial cooking session starts with you as the guide. If you remember something very specific from growing up and can attempt to recreate that dish, go for it!

---

[1] McDonough, Molly. "The Connections between Smell, Memory, and Health | Harvard Medicine Magazine." Magazine.hms.harvard.edu, Harvard Medicine Magazine, Apr. 2024, magazine.hms.harvard.edu/articles/connections-between-smell-memory-and-health.

A past client of mine often ate the same packed school lunch almost daily. For Jared, the BLT was a childhood lunch staple. This was a clear example of something he could recreate that would take him back to his childhood. The smell of cooking bacon reminded him of the family kitchen in his childhood home, and was the scent that often greeted him when he first woke up. The smell, taste, and texture of soft white bread spread with mayo, and topped with bacon, lettuce, and tomato, took him back to the lunch room, to the group of kids he sat with and the feelings that came flooding back as he remembered middle school.

If you are more comfortable starting slowly in the kitchen and taking baby steps, then a sandwich may be the perfect start for you. Feel free to channel the sandwich of your dreams and see how you can really get creative and represent a food memory in between two slices of bread. For example, if you remember mac and cheese, what cheeses were used? Could that dish be translated into some kind of grilled cheese sandwich?

Another client of mine remembered a stew that was a staple in his childhood home. He considered the ingredients that were in that stew and reconfigured them into a handheld meal. He utilized spices like curry powder and cinnamon and turned the chicken stew into a curry chicken salad sandwich. Remember, this session is focused on evoking smells and memory. Give some thought as to how to best conjure those up.

Now that you understand the reason for this first dish, let's talk about ingredients. There are many options and combinations. It's up to you to decide what to use. As you choose your ingredients, pick items that speak to you: ingredients that you like, something you remember being utilized often, something that was talked about in your home or that was presented regularly to you.

Maybe you are someone who struggles with this session because you didn't have a packed lunch, or you can't stand a meal you so often had to eat. This is an opportunity to repack those school lunches. What did you wish was in that brown paper lunch bag or lunchbox? Create that lunch and see whether it tastes as good as you once imagined it would taste.

Remember, there is NO right or wrong way to make this sandwich, or any sandwich! Your sandwich should be just as unique as you are. This dish should represent something about you and your early years of life. If you were telling a story to someone else about your childhood, what story would you tell? Try to use this meal to tell that story and why it is significant to the person you are today.

Below you will find a list of suggested ingredients divided by each element that goes on a tasty sandwich. You have several ways to proceed:

- You can choose one or none from each category.
- You can choose multiple ingredients from each.
- You can choose ingredients that aren't on this suggested list but are ingredients that were unique to your culture, ethnicity, or background.

You are in charge of your own sandwich just as you are in charge of your own memories... and your own life!

Your Sandwich

Recommended materials

Knife
Cutting board
Plate
Mixing bowl

Spoons, forks
Frying pan (optional)
Panini maker (optional)

Suggested ingredients

Breads
White, Wheat, Ciabatta roll, Focaccia, Pretzel, Bagel...

Protein
Turkey, Salami, Bacon, Tuna, Hard-boiled eggs, Sliced cheese, Peanut butter...

Produce
Tomato, Cucumber, Sprouts, Lettuce, Avocado, Onions, Celery...

Condiments
Mayo, Mustard, Ketchup, Pickles, Jam, Hot sauce, Pesto...

Goal Setting

What intention do you have for this session?

....

....

....

....

Name three condiments in your fridge right now:

1. ....
2. ....
3. ....

Name three common sandwiches you like:

1. ....
2. ....
3. ....

Name three types of bread:

1. ....
2. ....
3. ....

Consider the art of plating. How can you make your sandwich look visually appealing to you?

What is your sandwich strategy? What ingredients first come to mind? Are you taking risks with your choices or playing it safe?

Time to make your sandwich!

Once your sandwich is made and plated, take a bite. Be aware of the flavors and textures. Close your eyes and pay attention to what images, sounds, places, or people come to mind.

1. What sandwiches or other foods do you remember eating as a kid? Who made them? Who did you eat with? Did you enjoy those meals?
2. If you were anxious when you were a child, try to remember what made you feel uneasy. How old were you when this began? How did you cope with those feelings back then?
3. What support did you have then? Who helped you? If you didn't have support, how did you cope with your feelings?
4. Do you think you have learned different coping skills as an adult? Who supports or helps you now?
5. Are those feelings as a child different from feelings you have now or do they feel familiar?

Opportunities for the Future

Now that you have taken the stroll down memory lane, remember that our childhood foundation stays with us. It is our base for who we are and how we do things. Once you *understand* that foundation, then you have the *power* to decide what to stick with, what to change, and what metaphorical ingredients you select in each situation.

When faced with any life choices and challenges, ask yourself why you are making that choice. Are your early life circumstances contributing to your decision or your feelings or reactions about a situation in any way? Consider if your feelings are coming from a place of being triggered and taken back to those early years. Are you making a decision based on what was in your life back then or for the person you want to be today?

Reflection

Use this space to take notes on any ah-ha moments, things you'd like to remember later, things that may have surprised you, moments of clarity during this session, or any questions you have.

....

....

....

....

....

....

....

....

....

Next Session: Mindfulness

After you've spent some time reflecting on how your childhood affected your anxiety today, get ready to knead! Up next, we're making bread while practicing mindfulness.

Tentative date for next session: __ / __ / __

Chapter 4

Week Two: Marinate on Mindfulness

Making the Connection

Many skills in life build upon previous lessons and skills acquired. Culinary art therapy is no different. Last week, you began a wellness journey of self-discovery. Since the goal of this journey is for you to live a less anxious, happier life, you will see that you need to keep building on the skills offered in this book.

Last session, I asked you to make a sandwich. That sandwich wasn't only about the contents between two slices of bread. It was also a guided metaphor for you to look back into your early years and give thought as to where your sense of self came from. Hopefully, you were able to recognize some early patterns or reasons for how you got to the emotional place you are in now. Just like any other personality trait or characteristic, such patterns typically do not pop up out of the blue for no reason. We are born with a certain personality, but circumstances as early as infancy help shape us into the person we become. Anxiety has roots somewhere, and the more we can understand where those roots come from, the better off we are moving along on this wellness path.

In this chapter, we will keep moving forward on our journey to less anxiety and a happier life. This week we will explore the idea of mindfulness in and out of the kitchen.

Mindfulness—the idea of focused attention on the present moment and acceptance of our feelings, thoughts, and physical sensations—is a powerful way to lower anxiety. Meditation is probably the best-known way to practice mindfulness. You may have an image in your mind of a person sitting on a mat on the floor with their legs crossed, palms pressed together, maybe some gentle Zen music playing in the background. This person may sit in this pose for a few moments or maybe even hours. This certainly is one way to meditate, but it is far from being the only way to become more mindful.

For many people, reading a list of instructions, gathering ingredients, preparing the cooking or baking materials, and following a recipe step by step helps them to experience a Zen-like moment. It certainly takes much patience to be able to achieve a state of mindfulness, even while cooking.

Oftentimes, we become impatient in our day-to-day activities. We get agitated with certain situations or people, and these feelings result in a state of anxiety. Other times, we start off our day feeling anxious and, because of that, lack patience as we move along and make decisions throughout the day. Either way, this can be problematic if it is a regular occurrence. Prolonged anxiety can cause:

- insomnia
- fatigue
- trouble concentrating
- lack of motivation
- unhappiness.

Now we've set the scene, let's talk about how certain types of physical activity, such as making bread, can foster mindfulness.

Did you know that engaging in physical activity is good for lowering anxiety because the body releases endorphins (hormones) when engaged in pleasurable activities? These hormones help contribute to positive mental health. Typically, professionals will suggest physical activity like jogging or biking because these cardio activities increase your heart rate and allow for increased blood flow. But engaging in any physical activity that allows for your senses to get a workout can also be a boost to your mental health.

Engaging in breadmaking—waiting for the mixture to rise, kneading and rolling out the dough, and forming beautiful braided strands—forces us to pay more attention to the here and now, the present moment. It becomes more challenging to think back and remember what happened yesterday or this morning or to worry about what may be coming down the road tomorrow. Staying in the present is one way of keeping anxiety low.

Immersion in a baking activity of any kind takes the charged-up angst out of other thoughts and feelings, allowing us to feel calmer and more collected. You are focused on reading the recipe, following the instructions, being precise about your measurements, and combining ingredients. Baking takes concentration and close attention, but breadmaking, especially, has multiple steps in the process that require extra focus and awareness. Were you one of the millions of people during COVID who baked banana bread or tried making a sourdough starter for the very first time? I do not believe it is any coincidence that so many people took to baking when COVID lockdowns struck. People were scared, lonely, and deeply worried about what was to come. Breadmaking was the perfect way to distract, self-soothe, and ease some of that worry.

"By putting our attention on what we are thinking, feeling, and sensing, we remind ourselves that we are not our thoughts and feelings; there is a part of us that can observe them and let them go."

—Pauline Beaumont[1]

Now, I have a feeling I know what you are thinking here. "Julie, this sounds too easy. If it were really THIS simple, then why don't more people just bake bread to feel less anxious?" Well, I will tell you why it's not really that simple. We live in a world where we are used to doing ten different things all at one time. Even as I sit here and write this, I am:

- checking emails
- answering phone calls
- attending to my kids in the other room
- listening to people who are walking in and out
- hearing the news playing in the background

---

[1] Pauline Beaumont, *Bread Therapy: The Mindful Art of Baking Bread* (Yellow Kite, 2020).

- thinking about dinner that needs to be made
- petting dogs that want attention

and so on and so on.

While I hope you are reading this book and focusing solely on these words, that is laughably unlikely, and you are probably juggling a similar list to mine. We do not exist in a world where people are accustomed to or even comfortable with giving all their undivided attention to one task at a time. There are many wonderful aspects of living in this modern, technologically driven world; however, we also pay a high price for it.

To make matters even worse, I am doing all those activities simultaneously, as I am sure you are, too, and, well, those kinds of busy activities actually mask anxiety. If we are feeling anxious and we engage in one (or many more) of these tasks, they can certainly "take our minds off" of our troubles. But those other activities do not help us feel engaged and connected to our emotions so that we actually cope with our anxiety.

Breadmaking connects us to the moment and helps relieve anxiety by requiring our full attention. There are many skills that are needed in this process, and that means we need patience and opportunity to practice these skills. I know just the word "breadmaking" can cause even avid bakers to sweat, but I want you to keep in mind that the practice is what matters most, not being "perfect." Don't sweat it if your first loaf of bread doesn't come out completely perfect (it probably won't!), or your mind wanders to a work email you still have to send. Baking bread and becoming more mindful takes time and effort. But if you keep trying and you invest the effort, you will experience a payoff of both delicious bread and a quieter mind.

Andy was a recent client of mine who had sought out talk therapy for severe anxiety and depression. During an early session with me, he confessed he lacked motivation, and he was afraid everything would not be good enough. We talked it over: His anxiety was keeping him stuck. It was preventing him from taking action and from feeling capable of accomplishing anything worthwhile.

The next session, I brought in some vegetables, a knife, and a cutting board. As I assembled everything on the table, I told him, "We're going to try chopping as a way to learn about and practice mindfulness."

Andy threw me a very skeptical look.

"Here, I'll demonstrate for you," I said as I showed him how to chop, julienne, and mince.

He didn't move to pick up the knife. Instead, he said, "I'm not sure if I'm going to do it right." He stared down at his still-intact cucumber. "This feels so awkward."

"It is. Vegetable chopping in your therapy session is certainly not the norm," I said to validate his feelings and acknowledge this truly was something out of his comfort zone. "I believe you can give it a try and see how it feels anyway."

Then he took a turn and said nothing while he set out to reproduce my cucumber pieces. We were quiet and he paid attention to his grip, to the motion of the slice, to the pieces of cucumber. After a few minutes, he put the knife down and exhaled deeply and said, "I wasn't thinking about being anxious at all!" He recognized a much-needed respite from his anxiety and even felt ready to next try baking at home.

Learning to practice patience in order to achieve mindfulness is a skill that helps keep anxiety at bay. Cooking and baking both offer many opportunities to practice being patient and mindful. As we get started, it is important we put in a bit of effort to create the right kind of environment for us to be able to experience this meditative state. Before we start baking, let's set the stage for a positive experience.

We can create the right kind of environment in a few ways:

- **Clear enough time.** Make sure you've given yourself enough unhurried time to complete the recipe—don't forget prep and clean-up! Don't set yourself up for a stressful experience if you know you have too many other obligations at the same time or surrounding your desired cooking time. Choose a day and time when you have the possibility for success.
- **Get comfortable.** Make sure you are comfortable in your physical surroundings. Wear comfortable clothes that you're okay with getting messy or stained. You don't want to worry about ruining your favorite shirt, right? Set the air conditioning at a comfortable temperature or open a window, because you'll be turning on the oven soon. You might want to listen to your favorite playlist or a podcast.

- **Don't forget about any others who might need the space.** You might want to give a heads-up to others in the home and let them know you are in the space, or consider whether anyone will be needing a meal while you are working close by. If having your partner in the kitchen with you stresses you out, consider asking them if you can be solo in the space for a bit. Or let them know you're working on something and need some privacy.

- **Decide what distractions to limit.** Consider putting your phone on silent, or leaving it in the other room. Do you want the TV on or off? Can you put aside the laundry or other tasks that are calling out to you? Think of these distractions in a way that allows you to set boundaries around them during this unique time you are engaged in.

- **Set your intentions.** Be mindful of what your specific goals are for this recipe. Do you want to experience the act of breadmaking and just see what it feels like, or do you want to focus your attention on the level of mindfulness you can achieve, or do you expect to make the perfect braided loaf? Go into this session being realistic about what you would like to achieve and how you can work to reach that goal.

This week, you will be baking a sweet, simple bread recipe that is one of my favorites. I invite you to summon your inner yogi and enter your kitchen with the intention of being fully present, acknowledging any and all thoughts and feelings, engaging in the process, and seeing where it takes your anxiety level. When all is said and done, you'll get to enjoy a comforting slice of warm bread fresh from the oven.

Before you get started, be sure to take your time to read through the recipe and materials and ingredients lists. Gather any necessary ingredients and your baking journey will begin here!

Before You Begin, Consider This

As you embark on this bread recipe, check in with yourself. Take note of how patient you are feeling before you begin the process.

- Are you excited for this process?
- Do you feel pressed for time or comfortable with the time you have?
- Are you feeling preoccupied with other thoughts?
- Do you feel comfortable and confident focusing on the recipe at hand?

Take a few deep breaths before you assemble your ingredients. Set an intention for yourself so that you can feel focused and centered. This will also help you feel able to measure your success at the end of the experience.

Remember to keep the notion of mindfulness front and center in this session.

Pay attention to your thoughts and feelings and acknowledge them. Try not to dismiss the thoughts that enter your mind. Remember, there is no wrong way to experience this session. Whatever comes to your mind is perfectly normal. Notice your thoughts, and, as you acknowledge them, let them pass through your mind. Then, allow your mind and body to use all your senses. Be aware of what sounds, touches, and smells you are noticing. Allow your senses to be fully engaged in this process.

Appreciate the repetition of the activity. Similar to a workout, we count our movements or sets of intentional exercises. Try to apply that same concept to making bread. How many times do you knead the dough and then turn it, and then repeat?

Plan for the wait time in between rises. What plans do you have for yourself while you are waiting? Consider what you would like to do with that downtime and how you will feel during the wait. Try listening to a podcast, playing some music, sweeping the floor, or perhaps tending to a part of your kitchen that has been calling out to you for help getting organized or cleaned up.

Be sure to manage your expectations. Breadmaking is an art form. Your braided loaves may not look perfect the first time or even the fiftieth time. It is about the process, not only the finished product. How will you manage your expectations about your bread? How do you typically cope with imperfection?

Challah

Recommended materials

Yields 4 loaves

Large mixing bowl
Measuring cups and spoons
Thermometer
Stand mixer with hook
attachment (optional)
Meat thermometer
(optional)

Large mixing spoon
Plastic wrap
Knife
2 standard-size cookie
sheets
Parchment paper

Ingredients

5 tsp instant yeast
1¾ cups warm water
4 tbsp sugar
2 eggs
7 cups bread flour
½ cup honey

1 tbsp salt
½ cup olive oil
Nonstick cooking spray
1 egg, for egg wash
2 tbsp sesame seeds
(optional)

Directions

Active time: 20 minutes to make dough + 30 minutes to braid and get dough ready for the oven

Wait time: 1–2 hours for dough to rise

Bake time: 30 minutes for 4 loaves

This recipe can be made by hand in a large mixing bowl, or if you have a stand mixer with a dough hook attachment, that works well, too.

1. Combine yeast and warm water in the bowl, add in the sugar and mix for a few seconds. Make sure your water is the right temperature. If it is too cold, the yeast will not bloom. If it is too hot, the yeast will die. I like to use a meat thermometer to make sure it is about 100 °F before using. Allow the mixture to sit for a few minutes until it starts to bloom. It will look a little foamy and bubbly.

2. Add the eggs, flour, honey, salt, and oil. Turn the mixer on low speed, and gradually increase the speed until all the dough forms one ball and the sides of the bowl are clean.

3. If you are not using a mixer, you can make the dough with just your hands. Combine the yeast, warm water, and sugar in a large mixing bowl. Allow the yeast to bloom the same way as above. Then add the eggs, flour, honey, salt, and oil. You can use a mixing spoon to combine well, and then use your hands to make sure the dough comes together into a ball. On a clean work surface, use the palm of your hand to press the dough, folding it in and continuing to press with your palm. This motion is the kneading of the dough. Repeat for about 5 minutes until the ball of dough is smooth and not sticky.

4. Remove dough from the bowl and spray it with nonstick spray. Place dough back in the bowl and cover with plastic wrap. Allow the dough to rise for about 1–2 hours.

5. Flour your work surface with a few spoonfuls of flour. Using a knife, divide the dough into four sections. Each section of dough will make one loaf.

6. Using a quarter of the dough at a time, divide into three equal parts. Roll out each piece like a snake or strand on your work surface. Place three stands next to each other and press the top ends together. Braid the strands as illustrated below and pinch together at the end.

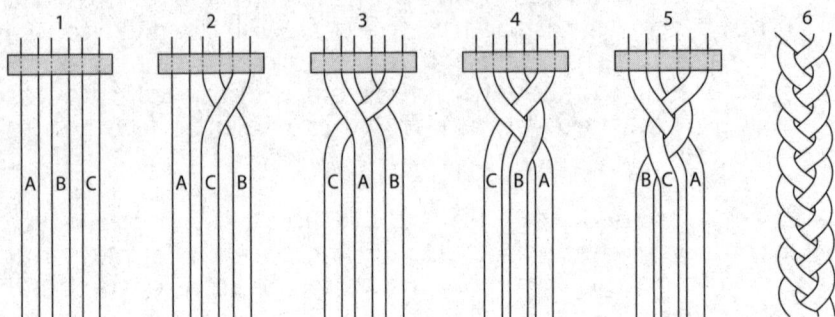

Place on a baking sheet lined with parchment paper. Roll the next three strands into snakes and braid them together. Place on the baking sheet. Repeat with the rest of the dough.

Allow the braided challah loaves on the baking sheet to rise for 1 hour. Then brush with egg wash and sprinkle with sesame seeds. Bake at 375 °F for about 17 minutes. Serve warm right out of the oven, or, when cold, slice for French toast or sandwiches.

Goal Setting

What intention do you have for this session?

....

....

....

....

Name three types of bread:

1. ....
2. ....
3. ....

Name three types of spreads that go on bread:

1. ....
2. ....
3. ....

Name three kitchen utensils you will use to make bread:

1. ....
2. ....
3. ....

Time to bake challah!

Once your bread is baked, cooled, and complete, think about your plans for this delicious treat. Would you like to share with a friend or neighbor, or would you like to slice a loaf and keep your pantry stocked for upcoming sandwiches or recipes? Remember that this is the outcome of your hard work and effort. You are in control of the next steps and the decisions you make about how to use it and who to share it with, or not.

1. Finally, how did the breadmaking go? How would you rate your experience?

Too challenging/ a total flop		Felt like a workout		Sense of accom- plishment/calm
1	2	3	4	5

2. As you were following the recipe, where did you notice your thoughts going? Were you focused on the task or other aspects of life?

3. Did you find yourself in the present moment or thinking about something outside of that moment? What did you do with those thoughts?

Opportunities for the Future

Now that your dough is made, kneaded, risen, braided, and baked, it's time to apply those actions and lessons to life outside the kitchen. Finding small moments or pockets of time to incorporate mindfulness into your daily routine is what will allow you to create a long-term ability to benefit from this practice and keep your anxiety low.

While baking bread there are many moments for you to pause and become aware of your thoughts, surroundings, and intentions. The more often mindfulness is practiced, the easier it becomes to find opportunities for mindfulness outside of the kitchen.

1. *Think of all the repetitive actions you do in your daily life. How often do you set an intention for those actions?*

....

....

....

....

2. *How can you carve out small moments to stop what you're doing and notice why you are doing those things? Or how can you acknowledge your thoughts and feelings more often without allowing them to define you?*

....

....

....

....

3. *Can you plan for the downtime in between actions? If you are driving a carpool and shuttling kids back and forth between locations, what can you do for 5 minutes for yourself to feel some calm?*

....

....

4. If you are working on a project in the office and are waiting for feedback from a boss or colleague, what can you do with that wait time to ease your anxious thoughts? Think about that wait time between rises with the bread. What choices and actions did you take then that can be taken in life outside the kitchen?

Reflection

Use this space to take notes on any ah-ha moments, things you'd like to remember later, things that may have surprised you, moments of clarity during this session, or any questions you have.

....

....

....

....

....

....

....

....

....

....

....

Next Session: Communication

Now you know what mindfulness is and how to incorporate it in your daily life, we're going to tackle communication. As you're going to learn, having hard conversations with your sous chef can be excellent practice for hard conversations with your coworker, family member, and others in your life.

Tentative date for next session: __ / __ / __

Chapter 5

Week Three: Communication— You Chop, I Stir

Making the Connection

Have you ever experienced the frustration of trying to tell a friend a story and the right words just weren't coming out the way you intended? Or perhaps a conversation with a loved one was getting heated, and you became overwhelmed and shut down rather than feeling able to express yourself adequately, enabling you to resolve the conflict. Did you feel your blood pressure rise? Your face get red? That feeling, if experienced often enough, can lead to anxiety.

Anxiety symptoms like racing thoughts and unorganized speech can also lead to poor communication, which can worsen mental health struggles. Communication and anxiety tend to be a chicken-and-egg situation. It can be hard to decipher which comes first. The good news, though, is that if you are aware of your communication style and how anxiety plays a factor in your communication, you can make an effort to modify your style and learn how to express yourself, your feelings, and your needs in the most helpful, productive way, leading to lower levels of frustration and anxiety.

When we talk about communication, it is important to recognize that communication is more than just the words you use. It also involves nonverbal communication. This includes things like:

- eye contact
- arm and hand gestures

- facial expression
- tone of voice
- posture
- the distance between yourself and the person you are talking to.

All these things convey a message, and it is important to be aware of what that message is and of how someone else may perceive that message and you.

Anxiety undoubtedly impacts your conversation skills. It may be difficult for you to start or maintain a conversation. You may find yourself talking too much, which can negatively impact others and how they interact with you. You may find yourself unable to speak clearly at all, which can lead to isolation and feelings of loneliness if you shut down and start disengaging from people in your personal or professional life.

Anxiety can have an intense impact on your relationships by making you overthink and dwell on negative interactions. You may become hesitant to express how you feel to the people that matter most. Anxiety can also make it difficult to truly listen to others in your life. All of this can lead to even more conflict and stress and hinder meaningful connection.

The Importance of *Why*

When communicating with a partner, a parent, a child, a coworker, or a friend, it is important to consider the value of *why*. Take a moment to differentiate between these two statements:

"I'm sorry, I can't talk to you right now. I am leaving the house."

versus

"I'm sorry but I don't feel able to have this discussion right now. I feel overwhelmed and nervous about the way this conversation may go. I'm going to leave the house and go for a walk so that I can collect my thoughts and prepare for our conversation."

In the first statement, it is unclear what the speaker's *why* is. In the second statement, it is very clear that the speaker is feeling nervous about the conversation and that they have a need they are trying to meet. There is a defined reason as to why they are leaving the house and where they are going.

You can reasonably guess that the person listening to this first statement may feel confused or even angry that the speaker is leaving the house. The listener is probably left with more questions than answers. This listener may respond with anger or they may shut down. The listener in the second statement has an explanation. The listener may not like what the speaker said but they have more information to process and understand. This listener may feel more patience or empathy and may respond with kind words rather than angry words.

Ultimately, the way we communicate with the people in our lives impacts us for the better or for the worse. If the speaker in either of these statements is experiencing anxiety, they deserve to be met with empathy, patience, and understanding. For people to give those things back to us, understanding the *why* is crucial. Providing that *why* can only come from one person, and we must decide how we can communicate in a way that can provide this information, allowing others to treat us in a way that can help us manage our own feelings.

Both statements may come from the same person in the same situation with the same feelings. But the second statement offers the listener a reason why. As we take a deeper look at your communication style, and as you practice communicating with this recipe, try to keep the whys in mind so that your communication can be successful.

Are you aware of your *why*?

Are you sharing your *why*?

Do you believe your *why* matters?

In this next session of cooking, I'm going to ask you to think about your style of communication and how you would like to experience this session. Let's begin by taking a deeper look into your own style of communication. According to many communication experts, most people's communication style will fall under one of four categories. It does not mean that one person uses only one of these styles all the time, but you will be able to see patterns for yourself and hopefully gain insight into how you communicate and learn more about why you communicate the way you do.

Four types of communication

Passive communicator

Hard time expressing feelings or needs

Quiet or shy

Does not want attention

Struggles to share needs or feelings

Hard time saying no to others

Perceived as easygoing

Avoids eye contact

Aggressive communicator

Often dominates conversations

Reacts before thinking

Intimidating

Interrupts others

Overbearing

Intense eye contact

Passive-aggressive communicator

Words and actions do not often match

Manipulative

Sarcastic

Talks under their breath

Has a happy face, even when upset

Assertive communicator

Friendly

Collaborative

Shares needs and feelings

Understands boundaries

Shows respect to others

Is respected by others

Appropriate eye contact

Evaluate Your Communication Style

Now that you have had a chance to learn more about these four different communication styles, think about how you communicate in your day-to-day interactions. It is important to understand your own style of communication, and how this style helps you and/or hinders you. Before you can make any meaningful or necessary changes, you need to examine your own choices and style.

1. Think of someone whom you interact with regularly—a partner, spouse, friend, or coworker. Can you identify and circle which style of communication you typically use with this person?

   Passive   Aggressive   Passive-aggressive   Assertive

2. Think of a specific conversation you have recently had and write down the words you used in this interaction. Take a moment to reflect how those words helped you or hindered you:

....

....

....

....

....

3. From that same conversation, consider which words and which communication style you would like to incorporate into this conversation in the future:

....

....

....

....

....

The kitchen is an ideal place to practice communication skills. There are clear tasks that need to be accomplished in a recipe, and there may be multiple ways to accomplish each task, but there are finite options for each task. If you are cooking with a partner, engaging with one another is vital. Otherwise, the recipe may not get accomplished or it may not be successful. The success of a dish isn't exactly vital, which can be reassuring, but it is a great way to gauge if you have been successful in your communication.

Have you ever heard or seen a chef operate in a professional kitchen? When the chef gets an order, they read it aloud with conviction and the others around them respond to that order with a loud, clear, and assertive "Yes, Chef!" Keep that in mind as you move forward with the recipe in this chapter.

"One of the delights of life is eating with friends, second to that is talking about eating. And, for an unsurpassed double whammy, there is talking about eating while you are eating with friends."

—Laurie Colwin[2]

2 Laurie Colwin, *Home Cooking* (Fig Tree, 2012).

Before You Begin, Consider This

Before you tackle the recipe in this chapter, decide whether you would like to cook with a partner and share the meal with them or cook solo and then invite someone to eat the finished meal with you. Some questions to think about:

- Which of these options would be the most beneficial and impactful for you?
- Would you like to share a cooking experience with another person?
- Is this the right opportunity for you to practice your communication skills?
- Would you rather cook on your own and invite someone to share the meal you already prepared?

If cooking with a partner:

- Ask your partner what ingredients they would like to use. Be mindful that you are a team and may not always agree on ingredients. How will you communicate if there is a difference of opinion?
- Discuss how you will divide the recipe tasks. Pay attention to what each of your prefer and how to share with your partner your own needs as well as listen to what their needs are.
- Talk about what is working, as well as what challenges you are managing. Be sure to celebrate your successes as well as any challenges you overcame.
- Communicate your *why* to your partner.

If cooking solo and presenting the dish to a guest:

- Start off by expressing appreciation for your guest joining you. Be sure to introduce the dish and talk about what the experience was like for you.
- Share the reason why you made this dish for your guest.
- Ask your guest about their flavor preferences or cooking experience. Remember to engage them in conversation in a way that is meaningful for them as well.
- Tell your guest what went well for you with this recipe and talk to them about what challenges you faced and how you managed them.

Sushi Bites

Recommended materials

Assorted small bowls
Plastic wrap
Serving plates
Rice cooker (optional)
Two sharp knives

Two cutting boards
Chopsticks
One small pot and lid
Empty egg crate
Peeler

Ingredients

Choose as many or as few as you would like:

Avocado
Cabbage, shredded
Carrots
Crab
Cream cheese
Cucumbers
Edamame
Green onion
Jalapeno

Lox (brined salmon)
Mango slices
Mayo
Seaweed
Sesame seeds
Sriracha
Sushi-grade fish
Sushi rice
Tofu

Step 1: Prep all the ingredients

Mise en place is a French term that means "everything in its place." This is how chefs prepare and line up all the ingredients required before cooking. The key is organization and order to help the chef feel a sense of control and readiness. This requires lots of communication in the kitchen.

1. Let's begin by cooking the short-grain sushi rice, according to the package direction. Allow time for the rice to cool before handling it and using it in the sushi bites. You want the rice to be at room temperature for this dish, so I would suggest cooking your rice at least 1 hour before assembling the sushi bites.
2. Slice the cucumber, carrots, mango into thin julienne strips.
3. Chop the cabbage into short thin strips as well.
4. Shell the edamame in a small bowl.
5. Slice the green onion into thin slices. Place in a small bowl.
6. Slice the jalapeno into thin round slices. Discard the seeds for a milder pepper heat. Place in a small bowl.
7. Peel the avocado and use a peeler to slice super-thin slices.

Step 2: Assemble the sushi

1. Start off by wrapping a piece of saran wrap around an egg crate.
2. Place a small amount of avocado first, then fish, then whichever other toppings/veggies you choose.
3. Finish each bite with a small spoonful of sushi rice that you pack and press in each piece tightly. This will ensure each bite stays neatly packed, making it easier to serve and eat.
4. Carefully flip over onto a plate or cutting board, and everyone can take a piece of sushi. Repeat for more bites.

Goal Setting

What intention do you have for this session?

....

....

....

....

....

Name three types of sushi:

1. ....

2. ....

3. ....

Name three types of sauces that are used with sushi:

1. ....

2. ....

3. ....

Name three kitchen tools you will use to make sushi:

1. ....

2. ....

3. ....

Time to make Sushi Bites!

- Did you remember to use the skills you practiced from the previous session? Were you able to be mindful and present while communicating at the same time?
- Which communication styles did you naturally find yourself leaning toward while in the kitchen? Is this similar to your communication style outside of the kitchen?

Opportunities for the Future

Now that you have cooked with someone else or perhaps shared what you cooked with someone else, think about how you communicated throughout this experience.

1. What worked and what was challenging?

....

....

....

....

2. Which was harder for you: to share your own needs or to be flexible and accommodate the other person's needs?

....

....

....

3. Can you think of a situation in your life outside the kitchen where you have experienced something similar?

....

....

....

....

4. Try to identify one area of strength for yourself with communication. Think about communicating with your family, friends, or coworkers. How have you seen that strength work to your benefit?

....

....

....

....

5. Now consider an area of communication that you struggle with. Was it the same in the kitchen?

....

....

6. How did you press forward in the kitchen with that challenge? What choices did you make in the kitchen (to cook solo or with someone, to talk or to listen) and think about which choices you can use at home or work?

Reflection

Use this space to take notes on any ah-ha moments, things you'd like to remember later, things that may have surprised you, moments of clarity during this session, or any questions you have.

....

....

....

....

....

....

....

....

....

....

Next Session: Problem Solving

As we'll cover in the next chapter, you should tackle one problem at a time. Use the next few days or week to think about your communication style and how you engage with others. And then, when you're ready, let's start problem solving in the kitchen!

Tentative date for next session: __ / __ / __

Chapter 6

Week Four: Problem Solving— No Pasta? No Problem!

Making the Connection

One of the hallmark traits of generalized anxiety disorder (GAD) is uncontrolled worry. Everyone worries—it is a part of life—but people who are anxious are typically spending a lot of their time worrying, far more of their time. If this is you, you might be confusing your ruminations and worrying with problem solving. When something becomes a habit, it is easy to mistake that habit for something else. Worrying is not the same as problem solving. Let's delve in a little deeper to understand the differences.

The *Oxford English Dictionary* tells us that *worry* is defined as "giving way to anxiety or unease; allowing one's mind to dwell on difficulty or troubles." It's that dwelling that people confuse with problem solving. People often think that good problem solving takes time. And certainly worriers are spending lots of time on a problem, so this must mean they are problem solving with all this worry. In fact, there is research that says that people worry because they think they are in fact problem solving.[1]

However, problem solving does not need to take days, weeks, or months, and prolonged worry actually makes us feel worse. Feeling bad for long enough periods of time can influence our judgment and decision-making ability. A negative frame of mind can

---

[1] Elizabeth A. Hebert, Michel J. Dugas, Tyler G. Tulloch, and Darren W. Holowka, "Positive beliefs about worry: A psychometric evaluation of the Why Worry-II," *Personality and Individual Differences* 56 (2014): 3–8.

make us feel more pessimistic about the problem, and more likely to dismiss any solutions we come up with as not good enough. Excessive worrying also has a significant negative impact on confidence. (We'll talk more about that in Chapter 9.)

So now that we know how common worrying is for people with anxiety, let's take a closer look at why problem solving is so important, especially for those struggling with anxiety.

Problem solving, done well, can lead to:

- optimism
- hope
- self-esteem
- self-assurance.

These all then lead to improved mental health and an overall happier life. Hello, jackpot!

When we feel all these things, we are able and better equipped to continue to manage all the stressors that come our way in life. Let's face it, stress and problems will always manage to creep into our world; it's a part of life for all of us. Knowing how to manage, solve, and handle these problems and stressors is what really makes the difference.

Don't forget, there are benefits to being a top-notch problem solver as well. Once you can keep that pesky anxiety in check by building more effective problem-solving skills, you may also find yourself able to get more creative and think out of the box at home or at the office. You may find yourself working better under pressure and not wanting to bury your head in the sand. Once the anxiety can be managed, there are so many more opportunities waiting for you.

Now that we know that worrying about a problem isn't the same as problem solving, and we know more about the benefits of becoming a rock-star problem solver, it is crucial to ask ourselves: How do we problem solve?

Consider these five stages when tackling a problem to solve:

1. Clearly pinpoint and define the problem.
2. Determine your goal for a solution.
3. Brainstorm all possible solutions.

4. Weigh the pros and cons of each solution.

5. Identify the best solution.[2]

So if we know that problem solving is not the same as worrying, and we now have a step-by-step formula to help us with productive problem solving, we can look to see how the kitchen can be a great playground for practicing problem-solving skills. There is great potential for finding small solutions to small problems in the kitchen. Replacing or substituting ingredients, modifying a recipe's cook time, and presentation are all possibilities that could solve a cook's problem.

Example from My Own Kitchen

Just last week, I encountered a kitchen problem of my own. I typically keep my freezer stocked with challah bread (Chapter 4). This bread is eaten in my home every Friday night as part of our sabbath meal. Last week, I opened the freezer and realized I was all out of bread.

The problem: It was Thursday afternoon, and I needed the bread for the next day. Typically, I would just make a fresh batch in the morning, but I had a full day, and I knew there would not be enough time to make the dough, let it rise, braid it, and bake it. This was my defined problem: when was I going to find the time to bake?

The goal: My goal was simply to have challah bread on the dinner table the next night.

The brainstorm: In my head, I came up with three options. I could change around my appointments the next day; I could buy bread

2 T. J. D'Zurilla and M. R. Goldfried, "Problem solving and behavior modification," *Journal of Abnormal Psychology*, 78(1): 107–26. https://doi.org/10.1037/h0031360

in the morning; or I could make the dough the night before and set it in the fridge to slowly rise overnight.

Weighing the options: I weighed all these options. Clearly, my day would be easier if I just bought the bread. I would give myself more time and less stress to have over my head. But I also knew my kids would be disappointed with the store-bought bread.

The best solution: I came to the conclusion that the best solution would be for me to take ten minutes Thursday evening and make the dough and leave it in the fridge overnight to rise. I came to terms with my answer after working through all possible solutions, and I settled on what worked best for me. Once I worked through this process, I let go of the stress and the choices and just did what I knew I needed to do to get the job done.

The challah may not have been my very best batch because of the timing of the rises and rest time; however, the challah made it to the dinner table the next day. No one paid attention to the specific consistency of the bread or compared it to the loaf the week before; they just knew they had homemade bread, and everyone was happy.

The best part of practicing problem solving in the kitchen is that if your recipe doesn't turn out well or even if it is a complete disaster, it really isn't the end of the world. Every recipe offers an opportunity to find solutions to safe, nonconsequential problems. The more proficient you become at solving cooking problems, or even just being more comfortable with the idea of managing a problem, the easier it becomes to find solutions to larger, actual problems in life outside of the walls of your kitchen.

Example from Outside the Kitchen

Just as I had the opportunity to work through a kitchen problem, at the same time, real-life problems arise all the time. It takes some practice to see these situations as an opportunity as well as a problem. The challah bread problem may have been solved, but the real-life problem for that day was that I am only one person and can only be in one location at a time.

The problem: So when an appointment gets scheduled, a friend calls to have a lunch date and dinner also needs to get made. I can see this as one large problematic day or I can see this as an opportunity to practice my problem-solving skills. My defined problem here is that I am only able to be in one place at a time and I cannot add hours to the day, no matter how much I wish I could.

The goal: I have to choose my priority and decide what will get done on any one particular day and what will have to wait. My goal for the day is to get done the things that need to happen—like get dinner made and pick up my kids from school. Whatever else I am not able to get to will wait for the following week.

The brainstorm: When I was brainstorming all the ways I could get my shopping and cooking done in addition to any other tasks that I needed or wanted to do, I could see I had options:

- I could make a dinner that was complicated and more time consuming.
- I could stick to what I know.
- I could consider what was in the fridge already and skip the store to have lunch with a friend.

Weighing the options: I weighed the pros and cons of getting to the store versus making a fridge-dive dinner. I considered taking the time to meet a friend versus putting that off and allowing more time to cook. I weighed how I felt and what I needed at that moment as well as what my family needed. I determined that no one else would know if I roasted the vegetables from the crisper or used vegetables purchased fresh.

The best solution: I needed some time to connect with a friend and I chose to skip the store that day. The best solution in that moment was to recognize that my family would eat, everyone would be taken care of, and I also deserved to have some time for myself to relax and connect with a friend. I let go of the other scenarios, and I allowed myself to enjoy my own choice knowing that everyone and everything would work out just fine.

Consider the kitchen your laboratory for problem-solving practice. Once you feel you are able to practice and master problem-solving skills, you will find less of a need to worry, thus eliminating or diminishing a major symptom and element of anxiety. Remember, this is a skill that takes practice, and with each recipe you have an opportunity to identify a possible problem or challenge. Instead of worrying about that problem, you are going to identify the steps that are helpful to find a solution to that problem.

Before You Begin, Consider This

Take a look at the recipe for Baked Cheesy Quinoa with Pesto below, and consider any potential problems or challenges with this recipe:

- Do you own a blender to make pesto?
- Do you have enough time to make each element of the dish?
- Do you have quinoa in your pantry? Have you made it before?
- Would you rather use pasta or rice?

Give yourself a few moments to problem solve using the five stages listed above:

Identify and define a problem:

....

....

....

Determine what your goal is for a solution:

....

....

Brainstorm all possible solutions:

....

....

....

....

....

....

....

....

List the cons for each solution:

....

....

....

....

....

List the cons for each solution:

Identify the best solution:

Remember that problem solving in the kitchen is low steaks (pun intended). You can remember to laugh and not take these kitchen problems so seriously. We all need a reminder from time to time that not every problem in life is dire. Sometimes, problems are just small obstacles and will not have a tremendous life-altering consequence. Embrace the process and know that whatever solution you find or struggle with, all will be okay.

Baked Cheesy Quinoa with Pesto

Materials

Yields 6 servings

Medium pot
Mixing spoon
Large mixing bowl

Baking dish
Food processor or blender

Ingredients

2 cups cooked quinoa
½ cup ricotta cheese
1 egg
1 cup frozen spinach, thawed
and drained
10 cherry tomatoes, halved
2 cloves garlic, minced
½ tsp dried basil
½ tsp kosher salt
½ tsp pepper
1 cup mozzarella cheese,
shredded
¼ cup Parmesan cheese
3 tbsp pesto (see directions)

Pesto
(yields about 1 cup)
1 cup basil leaves, washed,
stems removed
3 tbsp pine nuts
1 tbsp fresh lemon juice
2 cloves garlic
½ tsp kosher salt
½ tsp pepper
¼ cup Parmesan cheese
¼ cup olive oil

Week Four: Problem Solving – No Pasta? No Problem!

79

Directions

1. Cook the quinoa and allow it to cool down, mix in a large bowl with the ricotta cheese, egg, spinach, tomatoes, garlic, basil, salt, and pepper. Mix in a quarter cup of the mozzarella cheese. Set aside.

2. Preheat the oven to 400 °F.

3. For the pesto, place the first six ingredients in a food processor or blender. Pulse until combined well. Pour in the olive oil and mix until smooth and creamy. You can add in the cheese and pulse, or mix by hand, or skip the cheese all together.

4. Spray a medium-size baking dish with nonstick cooking spray. Pour the quinoa mixture into the baking dish and cover with the rest of the mozzarella cheese and the Parmesan. Using a small spoon, dollop the pesto over the top of the cheese. Bake in the oven for about 15–20 minutes until all the cheese is melted and bubbly.

Name three types of starches:
1. ....
2. ....
3. ....

Name three types of cheese:
1. ....
2. ....
3. ....

Name three different nuts:
1. ....
2. ....
3. ....

Time to cook!

Now that your quinoa (did you use quinoa?) is cooked, you can take a moment to ask yourself: Did your solution work?

1. Was the problem actually a problem?

....

....

2. Did the problem feel any different to you in retrospect when you were done cooking?

....

....

....

....

3. Is it possible that any solution or change you came up with actually made the recipe better?

....

....

....

....

4. If the recipe did not work for you, how has your life changed because of it?

....

....

....

....

....

Opportunities for the Future

Now that you have tested the waters of problem solving in the kitchen, is it possible to recognize a shift that you could make in your thought process at home or work when it comes to problem solving?

1. What did you learn or recognize when you solved a challenge with this recipe? How did you feel? Was it easier or harder than you thought it might be?

....

....

....

....

2. How did you feel when the recipe was complete?

3. Think of a problem or challenge you face outside of the kitchen:

4. What opportunities can you come up with to consider as options for solutions to that problem?

5. Do you feel more prepared to use the five stages of problem solving with that problem?

Reflection

Use this space to take notes on any ah-ha moments, things you'd like to remember later, things that may have surprised you, moments of clarity during this session, or any questions you have.

....

....

....

....

....

....

....

....

....

Next Session: Stress and Time Management

Keep on working on your problem-solving skills, in the kitchen and outside the kitchen. Next up, time management, stress, and vegetable frittatas.

Tentative date for next session: __ / __ / __

Chapter 7

Week Five: Stress and Thyme Management

Making the Connection

In Chapter 6 we learned how worrying about a problem does not actually solve any problems. The longer we worry about that problem, the more stress we experience. The more stress we experience, the greater we struggle with time management. Another possible scenario is that, for those who find time management challenging, that alone may lead to greater amounts of stress. Prolonged periods of stress can then lead to anxiety.

When people are able to manage their time successfully, they often feel calm, accomplished, confident, steady. Managing time successfully also allows us to feel a sense of control over our lives and environment. And when we have this sense of control, we are able to keep anxiety at bay.

On the other hand, when we feel stretched too thin, or unable to manage our time, it can be hard to feel any sense of control, or to stay focused, or to feel relaxed. We may experience feelings of overwhelm, guilt, or shame, and, inevitably, increased amounts of stress. We are more likely to avoid healthy activities like sleep, eating healthily, and socializing when we feel heightened stress and anxiety. These poor choices only create more stress, pushing us into a vicious cycle that becomes a struggle to break.

Symptoms of stress and anxiety often overlap, and it may be hard to distinguish the difference between the two. Let's take a deeper look at both stress and anxiety to better understand them and know when we feel one or both.

The main difference is that stress occurs because of specific, external circumstances. For example, if you are moving house or changing job, or are preparing to give a big speech, all these things can cause temporary stress and varying symptoms like stomach pains, nervousness, worry, or a hard time sleeping. You will notice, though, that the symptoms will subside once the situation comes to an end.

Anxiety is the body and mind's response to that stress. Anxiety is internal and may not resolve when the circumstances resolve.

Here is a breakdown to better help you recognize the symptoms of each stress and anxiety and what they have in common as well as what is different between them:

Anxiety	Both	Stress
Internal response	Worry, appre-hension, tension headaches	External response to something specific in your life
Ongoing feelings of dread, worry or uneasiness that impact different aspects of your life	High blood pressure	Feelings resolve when the threat is over
Consistent even without an external threat	Loss of sleep	Can have a positive or negative impact on action
	GI problems	

Stress can be a reason for poor time management, or poor time management can cause stress and lead to anxiety if there is no intervention. Learning how to practice time management skills can be a challenge, especially when the outcome has real-life consequences on your career, your family, or your personal life. It's a challenge to find ways to strengthen these skills in a way that you can feel confident will not impact your life or the lives of those close to you.

However, spending time cooking is a great way to practice your time management skills in a safe, inconsequential way. By trying a new recipe and engaging in some self-reflection, you can identify personal stressors and the way in which you respond and manage that stress. Because it is common for people to feel stressed or anxious when they feel pressured for time, the kitchen provides a great place to give those skills a workout. You will have to juggle multiple elements of a recipe, which gives you ample opportunities to practice managing your time and recognize what makes you feel stressed. Once you consciously notice these things, you can more easily apply the learned skills to everyday life outside the kitchen.

Letting Go of the *Shoulds*

So often in my practice, I work with clients who come in and tell me the same thing. They are struggling with stressors in their life because they feel as though they should be doing something a certain way. They *should* make a certain choice, they *should* go to a certain place, they *should* be doing this, that, or the other.

The response that I offer is typically the same: "Why?" Just as we learned the value of *why* when we communicate in Chapter 6, the *why* here, too, is important for us to understand ourselves. Many times when the answer to something is "I should" it comes from a place of self-judgment or a fear that someone else will judge us. Now, don't get me wrong—of course there are times when we *should* do something. When we get into a car, we *should* wear a seatbelt. We *should* follow traffic laws—these are things that keep us safe and they have a reason for existing. We *should* be respectful and kind to other people—it is what makes us decent human beings. Now, let's take a look at some other *should* statements and decide what the answers could be.

I *should* wear a suit to my cousin's graduation dinner. I am assuming everyone there will be in a suit. It is the appropriate attire for these events. I hate wearing suits. I feel like I'm being choked. I'm uncomfortable and can't enjoy myself.

Below is an example of what your response could look like. Read the responses and then try to answer with your own.

Q: What is the reason to wear the suit?

A: Everyone else will be wearing suits. I don't want to draw attention to myself by standing out.

Q: What stress will this cause?

A: This will cause me a lot of personal discomfort, and I won't be able to properly focus on my cousin or the meal. Being uncomfortable will make me crabby.

Q: How might time management be impacted?

A: It will take me more time to get ready, and I might get stuck in rush-hour traffic.

Q: What might a solution be?

A: I can wear a sports jacket instead, which is dressed up enough to fit in without making me uncomfortable or irritable.

I *should* offer to babysit my friend's small kids. She is a single mom and has not been out of the house in weeks to see friends. I should be able to babysit and make dinner for my own family, finish my work project, and clean my house.

Q: What is the reason to babysit?

A: ....

....

....

....

Q: What stress will this cause?

A: ....

....

....

....

Q: How might time management be impacted?

A: ....

....

....

....

Q: What might a solution be?

A: ....

....

....

....

I *should* eat more kale. It's healthy and important to eat lots of green, leafy vegetables. Even though I dislike the flavor and it makes my stomach hurt.

Q: What is the reason to eat kale?

A: ....

....

....

....

Q: What stress will this cause?

A: ....

....

....

....

Q: How might time management be impacted?

A: ....

....

....

....

Q: What might a solution be?

A: ....

....

....

....

Now that we have looked at a few different kinds of situations, consider the role that stress and time management may play in all these scenarios. Can you think of other times in your life when you let the *shoulds* dictate a decision for you that impacted your stress or time management? How did that relate to your anxiety level?

Before You Begin, Consider This

After you have read through the entire recipe and the directions, consider addressing how to keep your stress level low while cooking and how to best manage your time in order to successfully complete the recipe. Remember to consider how stress and time management can impact you during this process. The following tools are intended to help you as you consider how to best move forward in this recipe process. There is no right way or wrong way, it is about what feels best to you as the chef. You are in control of the recipe and your kitchen. Use these tools to help you feel empowered with your plan of action.

Make a plan

It is important to remind yourself that things don't just magically get done. It would be great if you did have a magic wand to let things happen on their own, but that is not realistic unless you're living in a fairytale. In order to see a finished dish, you need to create a plan of attack. Some questions to consider:

- When is a good day or time to make this dish?
- Who will you be cooking for?
- Is your fridge stocked with the right ingredients?
- Is your kitchen stocked with the right cookware?
- What other elements do you need to create a helpful plan for you in this process?

Create the right environment

Environment means more than just the physical space that you are in. Clearly the cooking will happen in the kitchen, but what about other elements of your environment? Would it be helpful or more enjoyable for you to listen to your favorite music while cooking? Would you consider cooking with a partner? Do you need alone time? It's important for you to check in with yourself and know how you can set the stage to make yourself feel the most relaxed and ready to tackle the frittata.

Create a priority list rather than a to-do list

I know many people often feel that a to-do list creates a sense of failure if they can't add that little checkmark next to an item. The goal is not the checkmark; the goal is the system. If you can, think of it as prioritizing where you want to start and what you want to accomplish rather than placing the success on whether you got to complete the task. Remember that you are the creator and owner of any list. You get to be the one to decide what goes on the list and how many checkmarks are really necessary on that list.

Break down tasks into manageable steps — *mise en place*

The French term *mise en place* means putting things in place. When tasks are broken down and organized by smaller, single items, you will find yourself able to line up items that make up the sum of a project. Whether it's writing a chapter of a book at a time, or focusing on a single element of a recipe at a time, every project is only the sum of all its parts.

Ask for help

This applies to any and all projects in life. Consider what you need help with or what you can allow someone else to take off your plate and do for you. It is not about giving away the work; it is about knowing your own limits and talents and trusting that other people can help.

It took me some time to be able to recognize that it's okay to ask for help. I often find myself wanting to do it all in the kitchen because I enjoy the process. But at some point, I was able to recognize that asking my kids or husband to help me did not need to diminish my enjoyment of the tasks. In fact, it made things better because I did not feel as rushed or pressed for time. This way, I could actually enjoy the tasks that I was working on more by asking someone to help alongside me.

It can be hard to ask for help, but very seldom do we accomplish anything all by ourselves. Lean on your support system and let them help you in the process of accomplishing your goals.

Avoid perfectionism

There is no such thing as perfection. Perfect does not exist in the kitchen, and it certainly does not exist outside the kitchen. Practice makes progress, not perfection. Creating a recipe is a great reminder of this. If something comes out a bit too peppery, it's okay. You will always find someone who likes spice. The kitchen is a great place to practice avoiding perfectionism because everyone has their own preference when it comes to taste. Remember that perfection can be subjective, just like what is considered a good frittata.

Avoid the *shoulds*

Remember to avoid making judgment calls. It is important to check in your judgment and leave it outside the kitchen. Set aside any judgment that you worry others may show you. Focus on your own needs and wishes. You are in control of your own decision-making process.

See the task through until the end — don't give up

I promise you will feel a sense of accomplishment and pride when you complete a recipe, just as you will when you complete any other task. Sometimes knowing you pushed through, you worked hard, and you were okay accepting being temporarily uncomfortable pays off in the kitchen and out of the kitchen. Let the process happen, and see where it takes you once it's complete.

> *1. Identify what may cause you stress with this recipe.*
>
> ....
>
> ....
>
> ....

2. How will you manage your time?

Vegetable Frittata Topped with Basil, Lime, and Arugula Salad

Recommended materials

Yields about 6 servings

1 frying pan
1 spatula
2 large mixing bowls
1 pair of tongs
1 knife

Cutting board
Baking dish
Blender or food processor
Microplane

Ingredients

Frittata
1 tbsp olive oil
1 small onion, minced
2 cups Yukon Gold potatoes, chopped into small pieces, or 18 oz frozen hash brown potatoes
1 tsp garlic powder
1 tsp onion powder
½ tsp salt plus ½ tsp salt
½ tsp pepper
1 tsp paprika
6 eggs
¼ cup heavy cream
1–2 cups assorted veggies from your crisper

(e.g. spinach, peppers, broccoli, zucchini)
1 cup shredded cheese of your choice (optional)

Basil, Lime, and Arugula Salad
2 limes, zest and juice
1 tbsp Dijon mustard
2 tbsp honey
10 fresh basil leaves
½ tsp salt
¼ tsp pepper
⅓ cup neutral oil like avocado oil or vegetable oil
5 oz fresh arugula

Directions

1. Preheat the oven to 400 °F.

2. Sauté the onions in olive oil until translucent. Add in the potatoes, garlic powder, onion powder, salt, pepper, and paprika. Cook on medium-high heat for about 5 minutes until potatoes have started to become slightly softened and a bit browned. Turn heat off. Spray a glass dish or pie plate with nonstick oil. Pour potato mixture into the dish. Set aside.

3. Crack eggs in a mixing bowl. Mix well with a fork. Add in the cream and mix. Add in veggies, cheese, and the half teaspoon salt. Combine and pour over potatoes. Bake for 20–25 minutes until eggs are set in the center and look firm.

4. Meanwhile, zest and juice both limes into a blender. Add the mustard, honey, basil leaves, salt, pepper, and oil. Blend until thoroughly combined. Pour half the dressing over the arugula in a mixing bowl. Toss well. Serve alongside the warm frittata.

Goal Setting

What intention do you have for this session?

....

....

....

....

....

....

Name three types of lettuce:

1. ....
2. ....
3. ....

Name three vegetables:

1. ....
2. ....
3. ....

Name three ways to prepare eggs:

1. ....
2. ....
3. ....

Time to cook!

- What choices did you make while cooking? How did these choices impact your time management?
- Did you feel a sense of control or lack of control while cooking? What other feelings did this lead you to experience?

Opportunities for the Future

What element of this recipe was the biggest stressor for you?

....

....

....

....

....

Was juggling multiple tasks or timing the process more challenging? Why?

....

....

....

....

What cooking strategies did you utilize and how did they ease your stress level?

....

....

....

....

What strategies did you use in the kitchen that could be applied to life outside the kitchen?

....

....

....

....

Do you struggle with any of these tools outside the kitchen? Which tool could serve you best outside the kitchen?

....

....

....

....

....

Select one tool and write a few ideas you have for how you can utilize it outside the kitchen.

🥄 Make a plan

🥄 Create the right environment

🥄 Create a priority list rather than a to-do list

🥄 Break down tasks into manageable steps—*mise en place*

🥄 Ask for help

🥄 Avoid perfectionism

🥄 See the task through until the end—don't give up

....

....

....

....

....

....

Reflection

Use this space to take notes on any ah-ha moments, things you'd like to remember later, things that may have surprised you, moments of clarity during this session, or any questions you have.

....

....

....

....

....

....

....

....

Next Session: Relationships

Over the next few days or weeks, keep developing your problem-solving skills and the tools you first experimented with in the kitchen. Once you've had some practice with those, flip to the next chapter on relationships and a chicken noodle bake!

Tentative date for next session: __ / __ / __

Chapter 8

Week Six: Relationship Ragu

Making the Connection

Anxiety can impact and hinder the relationships you have in your life. When you experience anxiety, you may pull away and isolate yourself from others, which is counterproductive. Doing so will only lead to other negative symptoms and challenges. Other times, loneliness can lead to mental health and physical challenges such as increased inflammation which activates pain centers and triggers other neurological responses in the brain. Even those who are the most introverted still need a sense of connection and strong relationships of some kind.

The U.S. Centers for Disease Control (CDC) and the National Institutes of Health (NIH) both agree that promoting connection between people, avoiding isolation, and feeling a sense of belonging helps individuals avoid feelings of depression and anxiety. Cooking is a wonderful way to connect to people in several different ways. There are many opportunities to use the kitchen for forming connections: Baking treats to deliver to a neighbor; hosting a Sunday dinner; making a big pot of soup for a loved one who is feeling under the weather are all great examples of how time spent in the kitchen helps promote positive relationships, connections, and a sense of belonging.

Engaging in the cooking process with a friend or loved one is an obvious way to feed that social connection. It's a great way to use all the skills you have been practicing from previous chapters. It's a productive activity that allows for building trust and community as well as creating fantastic shared memories. Sometimes, it's even possible to connect with a loved one who is far away. If someone is not able to join you in your home kitchen, consider scheduling a time for a virtual cooking get-together. You may not be able to taste each other's efforts, but you will no doubt feel the connection and the warmth coming through the screen.

By investing in important relationships, we receive love and support. When we feel more loved and supported, we also feel more accepted, which can lessen our anxiety. The body releases endorphins during positive social interactions, much like the physical response we feel after a good workout. This is a simple way to feel a boost of happiness, while also reducing stress. That's one of the reasons why people who feel more connected to other people have lower levels of anxiety and depression.

COVID baking and cooking is another example of how connection works. During the intensely stressful time of the pandemic, cooking helped many people maintain a sense of connection. If you were following along on social media and joining in with all those making banana bread or a sourdough starter, you were probably able to keep some anxiety and depression at bay by investing in a like-minded community, even if it was only a virtual one. There is magic in the belief that someone else out there in this big world is doing the same thing as us. That feeling of having something in common with another person or group of people reminds us all that we are a puzzle piece that can fit with other pieces, and that feeling provides reassurance.

It is also possible to use a recipe as a way to remember a loved one. Sometimes loneliness strikes after the loss of a family member or friend. A recipe can help serve as a reminder to reminisce and recall special moments of joy in your life. Since the sense of smell conjures memories, that means cooking with loved ones is possible by remembering them, opening your mind and heart to those memories, and keeping a piece of them alive in your kitchen.

When you're in the middle of cooking, or ready to present a complete dish, try snapping a picture or two of your creation and sending it to someone you are thinking about. When you are connected and willing to let loved ones into your life, they can help support many of the healthy coping skills that we've looked at in the previous chapters. This will allow you to feel emotionally closer to people in your life. Feeling loved and supported increases feelings of happiness and reduces stress, anxiety, and depression.

Before You Begin, Consider This

As we have just talked about the importance of connection and investing in relationships, take a few minutes to think about who you would like to connect with. Think about someone in your life who you enjoy spending time with and feel close to, or someone who you would like to be closer with. Someone who makes you feel safe, who brings out positive qualities in you, or who has a positive outlook on life that you consider healthy and beneficial to you.

Once you have that person in mind, think about whether you would like to extend an invitation to them to cook with you in your kitchen. Do you want to partner on a shared cooking experience or would you like to cook on your own and invite this person to share in a meal together once you have prepared the dish for them? Remember to think creatively. If this person is not close by, can you extend a virtual dinner invitation? Do you want to cook on your own and then write a letter or record a voice note to send to a loved one about your experience? Keep in mind all the options and flexible ways that we know can exist when it comes to connection and relationship building.

If you are not sure where to start, or if you feel intimidated by the process or even that there is too much pressure on you to connect, remember it all starts with a simple conversation. What better way to begin a conversation than to talk about dinner? Talk about the recipe that is included in this chapter. What do you think about it? Have you cooked anything like this before? Are you making any changes to the dish? Once you open your heart and begin the connection, you will find it will get easier and feel more natural. Here are a few things to remember as you begin investing in this relationship.

Shared experiences create bonds

Cooking is an opportunity for shared experiences. Collaborating on a meal encourages communication and teamwork. Whether you're rolling out pizza dough with your partner, preparing a holiday meal with family, or experimenting with a new recipe with friends, the time spent together fosters deeper connections. These small moments in the kitchen add up over time and allow for stronger connections when the opportunities arise for more important or necessary support. Pizza night bonds can lead to other bonds that really count when you are in a time of need or when something significant occurs. It sounds like a simple way to grow relationships because it is that simple. Pizza night can lead to a holiday meal, which can lead to a birthday celebration, which can turn into a moment when someone is sick or in diffi-culty and needs help. Creating these small moments that allow people to bond can lead to larger moments that fulfill needs and offer moments of joy.

Building traditions

Food is often at the heart of many traditions. Passing down family recipes or creating new ones can build a sense of continuity and belonging. These shared rituals can become cherished memo-ries, strengthening bonds through the generations. Remember, even if you don't have traditions in your family right now, it is never too late to create some. Every tradition starts somewhere.

One of my favorite family traditions is our weekly shabbat dinner, or sabbath meal. Religious observance changes with each gen-eration, and what my family does may not look exactly the same as what my great-grandparents or even my grandparents did; however, there has always been a Friday-night dinner. My kids can count on that homecooked meal every single Friday evening. They know it begins with the lighting of candles and the bless-ing over wine and challah bread, and concludes with full bellies, good conversation, and a chance to connect and catch up on the events of the week.

I often talk about the times when my own family would sit around the dinner table and my grandma would look at me with a big smile and tell me how proud she was of me. For a long time, it confused me, almost insulted me. Why is she so proud of me serving chicken and roasted potatoes? I wondered. It was some years later that I realized it was not about the chicken and pota-toes; it was about me maintaining, protecting, and continuing this family tradition that is part of our legacy. Once I understood, it enabled me to feel an even deeper commitment and connec-tion to this tradition.

A safe space for vulnerability

The act of cooking allows us to be present, relaxed, and open. Conversation flows more naturally when chopping vegetables or waiting for a sauce to simmer. These acts of mindfulness allow us to be more present and calmer. This informal setting can encourage people to share their thoughts and feelings more freely and safely, deepening their connection with one another. Just like that teenager that talks more freely while sitting as a passenger in the family car, people open up more easily while engaged in a safe, low-stakes activity like cooking. Have you ever found yourself sitting in a staff meeting at work and doodling in a notepad, or cleaning the house while listening to a podcast or music? There is something about that slight, safe distraction that encourages more pathways to connect and deepens attention to a specific, desired task. Working to enhance your connection with a loved one or building a new connection with someone specific in your life can feel much easier when you are working on a shared task instead of a more pressure-filled, face-to-face assignment.

Relationship-building tips:

Open your mind and your heart.

Start with simple conversation starters.

Utilize the support from your cooking/dinner partner.

Remember to have fun — it's good to laugh and enjoy the process, as well as the food.

Chicken Noodle Bake

Recommended materials

Yields 6 servings

Baking sheet
Large pot
1 large mixing spoon
1 small mixing bowl
1 spoon

1 spatula
2 forks
1 knife
Cutting board
Baking pan

Ingredients

2 skinless boneless chicken breasts
2 tbsp + 2 tbsp olive oil
½ tsp kosher salt
¼ tsp pepper
¼ tsp granulated garlic
¼ tsp onion powder
¼ tsp paprika
1 onion, chopped
1 carrot, peeled and diced
2 stalks celery, diced

1 clove garlic, diced
4 tbsp all-purpose flour
3 cups low-sodium broth
1 cup cream/milk/almond milk
1 cup frozen peas
1–2 tbsp fresh parsley, chopped
8 oz egg noodles
1 cup panko breadcrumbs
Nonstick cooking spray

Directions

1. Preheat the oven to 425 °F.

2. On a baking sheet, drizzle chicken breasts with 2 tbsp olive oil, salt, pepper, granulated garlic, onion powder, and paprika. Roast chicken uncovered for about 25 minutes until cooked through. Once chicken is cooked, either chop it or shred it and set aside.

3. In a large pot of water, boil the egg noodles until al dente. Drain and set aside.

4. In the same pot in which you cooked the noodles, sauté the onion, clove of garlic, carrot, and celery. Season with a sprinkle of salt and pepper.

5. Once all the vegetables are tender and softened, add the flour and mix well. Cook on medium heat for 1 minute. Then add the stock and bring to a boil. Cook for 2 minutes to allow the sauce to thicken. Then add the cream/milk/almond milk. Cook for a few more minutes and then turn off the heat.

6. Add in the peas and parsley and cooked chicken. Mix well. Add in the cooked noodles. Then pour the entire mixture into a baking dish that has been coated with olive oil or nonstick spray.

7. In a small dish, combine the panko breadcrumbs with a pinch of salt and pepper. Add 1 tbsp olive oil and mix well with a fork. Spread the panko mixture over the chicken and bake uncovered on 400 °F for about 20 minutes until browned and crisp. Serve hot and enjoy.

Goal Setting

What intention do you have for this session?

....

....

....

....

....

....

Name three types of noodles:

1. ....

2. ....

3. ....

Name three ways to prepare chicken:

1. ....

2. ....

3. ....

Name three people you enjoy sharing meals with:

1. ....

2. ....

3. ....

Time to cook!

1. How did you decide who was going to prepare each item? Were tasks discussed or assigned?
2. Did you listen to music? What were the elements of fun that were part of the cooking experience?
3. Can you see any traditions evolving from this shared experience?
4. Think of one way you might feel slightly more connected to the person you cooked with or cooked for.

Opportunities for the Future

Most people wouldn't necessarily think of cooking as their go-to activity to spend quality time with someone else, but it is a great opportunity for connection since it generally happens multiple times every single day for your entire life. There are plenty of other opportunities for connection all around you, you just need to find them.

1. What other hobbies or interests do you have that could involve other people?

2. What are other frequent moments in your day when you think of other people in your life?

....

....

....

3. Who are the people that you are usually surrounded by? How can you reach out to one of those people and use those moments to connect with them?

....

....

....

4. Are you satisfied with the level of connection with them, or do you think you could implement strategies to deepen that connection?

....

....

....

Reflection

Use this space to take notes on any ah-ha moments, things you'd like to remember later, things that may have surprised you, moments of clarity during this session, or any questions you have.

....

....

....

....

....

....

....

....

Next Session: Self-Esteem

It takes time to build new relationships and strengthen existing ones, but keep at it and your life will be so much richer for it. But as you invest in your relationships with others, don't forget your relationship with yourself. We will cover this in the next chapter, along with some delicious cake!

Tentative date for next session: __ / __ / __

Chapter 9

Week Seven: Self-Esteem— Julia Child, Here I Come!

Making the Connection

You have now almost completed the eight-week program in the kitchen. I hope you are feeling proud of yourself at this point and acknowledging that when we feel good, we usually have less room for anxious thoughts. Living with chronic low self-esteem can be harmful to your mental health. Low self-esteem exacerbates doubts and fears, which leads to further avoidance of healthy behavior.

Cooking provides a low-risk, inexpensive, quick opportunity for a great self-esteem pick-me-up! Tackling any task where you can identify a concrete beginning and end and know that you accomplished something very tangible and specific can make you feel great. Take it a step further: Let others weigh in on your effort and this can take that self-esteem boost even higher. And what better way to enjoy a boost than with cake? Cake typically feels like a celebration, and sometimes a little celebrating goes a long way to make a person realize their own worth. Before we get to the celebratory cake, though, let's explore a bit more the impact self-esteem has on anxiety.

On an especially anxious day, do you feel like avoiding the decisions around making dinner as well as the actual process itself? This desire to avoid is very common for anxious people, and sadly it perpetuates their low self-esteem by reinforcing feelings of doubt, fear, and worthlessness. All those feelings play into the symptoms of anxiety.

But maybe your anxiety manifests differently; instead of avoidance, perhaps you shut down instead. This can look like refusing to take on a big or unknown challenge like making dinner or a holiday meal. You may be able to relate to this way of thinking: "If I can't make this recipe the way it is supposed to be, what is the use? I shouldn't even bother."

Well, I am here to tell you why I would like you to bother. If you can refrain from this all-or-nothing thinking, you will benefit from this recipe more than anyone else. Instead of thinking "Why bother?" try thinking "I'm going to try my best." Once you can find the motivation to simply try, make arrangements to lean on your support circle and allow yourself to listen and feel their gratitude and appreciation for your effort. You will feel a sense of accomplishment, no matter how much of a miss the recipe seems to you. This is the beginning of how cooking and baking can allow you to grow your confidence. Let's take a look at some other powerful examples of how cooking builds confidence.

Skill Development

As you learn, practice, and develop your techniques in the kitchen, you will be able to see for yourself the progression of a skill in an impactful way. Preparing a meal or mastering a new recipe boosts self-assurance by proving to yourself that you can, in fact, try something, accomplish something, and taste and smell your own development. There are not many tasks in life where some-one can so clearly see—and eat!—their own progress. Being able to experience this kind of skill development is a wonderful, con-crete way to boost your confidence.

Creativity and self-expression

The reason cooking is considered an art form is in part because it offers an outlet for creativity and self-expression where you can experiment with flavors, textures, and presentation. Expressing yourself through your food fosters a sense of individuality. You deserve to feel confident in your own uniqueness, and cooking is a fantastic way to be able to celebrate that individuality. This is crucial to understanding that there is no right or wrong in the kitchen. We all smell and taste in our own way. If something tastes or smells good to you, then it is done "right." Remembering to place the emphasis on cooking as a creative outlet instead of worrying about whether a recipe will come out correctly is imperative to enhancing your confidence.

Providing for others

Sharing dishes with friends or family creates a sense of pride and connection, as we already covered in the last chapter. Their positive feedback reinforces your ability to contribute meaningfully to their lives.

Have you ever volunteered for an afternoon serving others in some way? If you have done this, then I am sure you have walked away from that experience with your head held a little higher, standing a little taller. That is because you felt the benefit of knowing that you impacted someone else for the better. Being able to serve cake to a loved one may not be life changing. However, that small sense of being able to positively impact someone else is significant. It stays with you and helps motivate you to take future action steps. Each of these steps adds to your growing level of confidence.

Overcoming challenges

Attempting something new—something that challenges you—and learning from your struggles builds perseverance. Winning feels so good, it can be intoxicating. Sometimes we can find ourselves chasing the win just so we can feel good. The thing is, though, so often we actually learn more and grow more because of our failures, not our wins.

It's a tough fact to accept, but once we fully embrace the lessons we learn from challenges in the kitchen, we develop grit. When we take this grit out of the kitchen and into problems in everyday life, it builds our stamina, our sense of determination, and our resilience, all of which will pay off in many ways, especially by decreasing anxiety.

Independence

A sense of confidence is connected to our sense of autonomy. If you do not believe that you can accomplish a task, it is likely you are convinced that others think you are not capable of accomplishing that task. Those feelings lead to self-doubt, more negative beliefs, and more self-criticism. Those traits over time add up to a perception of worthlessness. What better way to show yourself how capable you are than by feeding yourself? You can taste the results for yourself and then take your hard work over to a friend or loved one and let them see, smell, and eat the results for themselves. This small accomplishment is a daily (three times daily actually) reminder that you are capable of being able to rely on yourself. Confidence starts by believing in yourself and showing others how they can rely on you as well.

You can see how cooking combines practical skills with limitless opportunity for exploration and personal growth, making it a rewarding opportunity to build confidence regularly.

One of my favorite success stories is about a client who I worked with for only a few sessions. Layla had this idea in her mind of what meals and other tasks needed to look like. So often Layla felt as though she was not living up to her own impossible standards. After these sessions, along with discussions and some food prepping, Layla realized that when she let go of her expectations and allowed herself to be more present in the moment and accept the praise from her loved ones as genuine, she was able to take in the appreciation and compliments and internalize those feelings as increased self-worth.

Before You Begin, Consider This

Oftentimes, I find myself walking into bakeries and taking in the beautiful works of art like someone who has just walked into an actual museum of art. I appreciate the skill and talent of those bakers who have worked so hard to create mini masterpieces made from sugar, butter, and flour. The amount of creativity, talent, and skill that goes into each confection never ceases to impress me. Now, I would never want to diminish or take away from the training and effort that those bakers put into their art. However, I think that anyone who puts their mind to creating something beautiful is capable of it. It may not be working with candy or sugar crystals, but I believe that anyone who has a desire to bake a cake can do it. You just need to believe you are capable.

The recipe that I am about to share with you comes from my grandma. She was a very talented baker who was famous for keeping a well-stocked freezer in case of any last-minute guests. She would never have found herself in the position of hosting someone and not being able to offer them a slice of her latest baked good. She had many family recipes and many newspaper clippings of recipes that she wanted to try and share with loved ones. One of her staples—and one she had famously perfected— was her marble cake. She used the most beautiful bundt pans, and her cakes were always so tall and luscious. To me, each one came out better than the previous one.

After she passed away, I held on to her recipe box (and folders and notebooks and clippings). Each recipe was a memento of her. Each recipe told a story to me. Each one had handwritten notes on them, or doodles of some kind that were reminders to me that they were hers and that each one mattered to her.

It wasn't until just a few years ago that I pulled out this recipe card for her famous marble cake. The recipe seemed so easy, just a few simple ingredients, yet I was nervous that I wouldn't be able to capture her exact flavor. I decided to persevere and give it a try. The cake came out well: a solid B+ for effort and taste. Everyone else was delighted as they sampled bites and remarked on my accomplishment.

I felt good that I had tried, but I was not yet fully satisfied. I swapped ingredients for brands that I knew she liked, and with a little more patience and effort each cake came out closer to hers. After making and remaking her recipe two or three times, I realized I was missing out. By being so focused on the small details of each element of the cake, I wasn't seeing the cake as a whole, as my grandma's cake. Once I was able to celebrate what was there instead of fussing over what was missing—focusing on the positive not the negative—I recognized my accomplishment and felt good. I felt more confident and I allowed everyone else's excitement to help me feel satisfied and self-assured.

1. Did you ever wish you could try something but you let something get in your way that stopped you from trying? What was it?

....

....

....

2. Can you think about a time you tried something that you were apprehensive about? How did it turn out?

....

....

....

....

3. How do you feel about baking this cake?

....

....

....

....

....

4. On a scale of 1 to 5, where is your confidence in baking?

1 Not confident at all   2   3   4   5 So confident

5. What do you need to feel more self-assured in this recipe?

....

....

....

....

....

6. I'd like you to think about a plan for your cake. Who will you share it with? When will you serve it? How will you handle the feedback from others about the cake?

....

....

....

....

....

Grandma's Marble Cake

Recommended materials

Bake time: 30–50 minutes, depending on baking dish size

Stand mixer with paddle attachment or a large mixing bowl

Spatula

1 small pot

1 small glass bowl

Bundt pan (you can also use a loaf pan and cut the baking time in half)

1 knife

Ingredients

1 lb butter

2 cups confectioner sugar

6 eggs

2 tsp vanilla extract

3 cups all-purpose flour

1 tsp baking soda

1 tsp baking powder

Pinch of salt

8 oz semi-sweet chocolate

1 tbsp heavy cream

Directions

1. Preheat the oven to 350 °F.

2. In a stand mixer with a paddle attachment, cream together the butter and sugar. Add in the eggs and vanilla. Mix well until thoroughly combined. Add in the flour, baking soda, baking powder, and salt.

3. Grease a bundt pan with butter and lightly flour. Using a spatula, pour the batter into the pan. Set aside.

4. Bring a small pot of water to a boil. Set a glass bowl on top of a pot. Make sure the bottom of the glass bowl does not touch the water. This is known as a "double boiler." Add the chocolate and heavy cream in the glass bowl and mix until melted. Pour the chocolate around the batter in the bundt pan. Use a knife to swirl the chocolate throughout the batter, creating a marbling effect.

5. Bake the cake for 50 minutes. Then turn the oven off and leave the cake in the oven for 10 minutes. Allow the cake to cool completely before removing from the bundt pan.

Goal Setting

What intention do you have for this session?

....

....

....

....

....

Name three types of cake:

1. ....

2. ....

3. ....

Name three types of frosting that go on cake:

1. ....

2. ....

3. ....

Name three kitchen utensils you will use to bake:

1. ....
2. ....
3. ....

Time to bake!

1. Now that you are aware of your confidence level going into this recipe, how will you be able to gauge your confidence level after baking? What will help allow you to feel more confident?

....

....

....

....

....

2. Think of a time in your life when you felt super confident. What contributed to your confidence?

....

....

....

....

....

3. Who is the lucky winner who you will share this cake with? How does this person impact your confidence level?

....

....

....

....

....

Opportunities for the Future

Oftentimes, we allow our fears or self-talk stop us from trying new things or activities that we tell ourselves we just can't do. Baking a whole, large, beautiful cake from scratch is something that many people would never even consider trying. But you are doing it!

1. When you accomplish a task, do you give yourself the pat on the back you deserve? How do you celebrate this?

....

....

....

....

....

2. When someone else offers you a compliment, how do you receive and process it?

....

....

....

....

....

I'd like to encourage you to find other moments of "cake baking" in your life. Find the tasks that just seem impossible or unlikely and give them a try.

Pay attention to the comments or remarks that others offer you when they give you praise or acknowledgment. We all need moments of recognition. They often come in different forms, but it is imperative that we notice them, accept them as true, and allow them to soak in.

Reflection

Use this space to take notes on any ah-ha moments, things you'd like to remember later, things that may have surprised you, moments of clarity during this session, or any questions you have.

....

....

....

....

....

....

....

Next Session: Choose Your Own Meal Adventure

In the next chapter, it's time to utilize all the skills you have learned in the past seven sessions and tackle a new recipe (and your anxiety) by putting them all together.

Tentative date for next session: __ / __ / __

Chapter 10

Week Eight: Choose Your Own Meal Adventure

Making the Connection

You have just spent the last seven weeks practicing and homing in on different life skills that will serve you well for many years to come. Each of these skills will improve your mental health and decrease the level of anxiety you experience. It is crucial to reflect back and take a moment to truly focus on what you have just accomplished. I hope you feel a sense of pride in yourself for seeing through the challenge you committed to. I know the process was most likely not always easy, but you did it and that is a great accomplishment. Even if each week did not look quite the same or feel the same, that is okay. The process is different for everyone because all of us are different.

For the past seven weeks, you have been busy learning to equip yourself with the practical tools and strategies that will better enable you to handle the common daily challenges each of us faces. By honing these skills, I hope you will feel a stronger sense of control and empowerment that ultimately will reduce fear, worry, and anxiety.

Give yourself a big pat on the back and enjoy a slice of the marble cake you made in Chapter 9!

Moving ahead now, this week I would like you to think about the skills you have already practiced. What was the most challenging? What came more easily to you? How did focusing on each of these skills impact you? Feel free to turn back the pages and reread your concluding reflections from each previous chapter. Use this space below to check in with yourself and see where your current anxiety level is related to each new skill.

Food and memory

1. What is something that continues to make you feel anxious about this topic?

....

....

....

....

2. What is something that you learned about this topic that eases your anxiety?

....

....

....

....

3. How can what you learned be applied to your everyday life outside of your kitchen?

....

....

....

....

....

Mindfulness

1. What is something that continues to make you feel anxious about this topic?

....

....

....

....

2. What is something that you learned about this topic that eases your anxiety?

....

....

....

....

3. How can what you learned be applied to your everyday life outside of your kitchen?

....

....

....

....

Communication

1. What is something that continues to make you feel anxious about this topic?

....

....

....

....

2. What is something that you learned about this topic that eases your anxiety?

....

....

3. How can what you learned be applied to your everyday life outside of your kitchen?

....

....

....

....

Problem solving

1. What is something that continues to make you feel anxious about this topic?

....

....

....

....

2. What is something that you learned about this topic that eases your anxiety?

....

....

....

....

....

3. How can what you learned be applied to your everyday life outside of your kitchen?

....

....

....

....

....

Stress and time management

1. What is something that continues to make you feel anxious about this topic?

....

....

2. What is something that you learned about this topic that eases your anxiety?

....

....

....

....

3. How can what you learned be applied to your everyday life outside of your kitchen?

....

....

....

....

....

....

Relationships

1. What is something that continues to make you feel anxious about this topic?

....

....

....

....

2. What is something that you learned about this topic that eases your anxiety?

....

....

....

....

3. How can what you learned be applied to your everyday life outside of your kitchen?

....

....

....

....

....

....

Self-esteem

1. What is something that continues to make you feel anxious about this topic?

....

....

....

....

2. What is something that you learned about this topic that eases your anxiety?

....

....

....

....

3. How can what you learned be applied to your everyday life outside of your kitchen?

....

....

....

....

Before You Begin, Consider This

This week, you will be identifying the area that you would like to continue to focus on, the skill that you feel needs more work. This may feel uncomfortable because I am asking you to lean into something that makes you uneasy. That is not a simple thing to do. It will take courage to face this challenge, this thing that you know you are still struggling with, and it may temporarily increase your anxiety in the short term.

Please keep in mind that it will get easier. Remember that you are in control of your own space and experience. In each previous chapter, we discussed the ways in which you could temper the experience to work for you. I would like to ask you to do the same thing now. Choose a skill that you would like to dig deeper into and learn more about, and continue the journey. Pick the time that works for you. Invite the appropriate people to join you, if that helps, or ask them to respect your privacy and space in a way that makes it easier and safer for you to move forward.

If you aren't quite sure what skill you'd like to focus on in this chapter, here are a few questions to help guide you:

- What would you like to cook? Is there a recipe or a dish that has been calling out your name? What life skills can you identify in the recipe?

- What opportunities do you have to practice patience and being present in the moment?
- What elements of communication, problem solving, stress or time management are needed in the recipe to make a successful dish?
- Will this recipe offer you an opportunity to connect to someone and strengthen a relationship? Or will you build upon last week's session and use it as a chance to keep working on raising your self-esteem?

There is no wrong recipe, and there is no wrong skill. You are the master chef here, in charge of your own kitchen, and you are the master of your own life as well.

For the last seven weeks, I have been your guide and your coach. I have been on the pages with you, guiding you along the way, and I hope you have felt that support. I am still here guiding you, but the training wheels are ready to come off. You are now ready for this next stage in this journey. I recognize that there may be a slight increase in anxiety as you feel more independence in this process, and that is perfectly okay.

This is when you take a deep breath, remind yourself of the skills you have practiced and learned from each week, and know you are ready to move forward. If the anxiety or doubt begins to creep in further, focus on these tips as a way to keep your attention on the skills that matter and will help you through the process.

Keep things simple

If you're new to meal planning, don't try to plan a ten-course, gourmet meal right now. Start with a simple recipe you have a desire to try, and even a sense of confidence with. Maybe you have made something similar before. Choose a simple recipe with familiar ingredients to build your comfort level. As you get more and more comfortable, you can gradually increase the complicating factors, flavors, or elements in a dish. This is all part of the process, and be sure to continue from a place that is the logical next step for you.

A flexible feast

A rigid plan can feel overwhelming and may trigger your anxiety. Instead, remember to consider flexibility when selecting your recipe. If you find a recipe that calls out to you but you are missing an ingredient or two, consider the ways in which you might be able to be flexible. Can you swap ingredients? Can you make time for a quick trip to the market? Is it better to switch recipes for now? A recipe is your guide in this process; you do not need to stick to the exact letter of the recipe. You are in charge of the recipe and how that recipe gets completed.

Consider your loved ones (or don't)

Give some thought to whom you would like to include in helping you with this dish. Or consider whether you would like to have the kitchen space all to yourself while chopping and mixing. There is no wrong way: It completely depends on the skill you are focusing on and the way that feels most comfortable for you to execute your plan.

Peek in your pantry

Having basic staples on hand will reduce stress when selecting the recipe and cooking your dish. Take a look in your pantry and see what ingredients you might already have on hand. Being able to see what you already have in stock may help you choose a recipe or at a minimum will make the shopping experience easier and less stressful if you do need to make a trip out to the market before cooking.

If your pantry needs restocking, flip back to Chapter 2 for a list of my recommendations for staples to keep on hand.

Use technology wisely

While I do love a good Pinterest recipe search, or visiting my favorite Instagram pages to get some inspiration for recipes, you want to make sure that the endless options on the internet do not overwhelm you, adding to any existing anxiety. Sometimes, having too many options is not helpful and can have the opposite effect to what we are looking for.

Be mindful of the role that technology plays while you are cooking. Consider putting your phone on "do not disturb" to avoid stress or unwanted distractions. Music or a podcast, however, might help you feel more relaxed and have fun with the process.

Give yourself grace

This tip may be the most important of all. Keep in mind that no plan is perfect and no recipe is perfect because we are not perfect either! Chances are that something will send you for a loop or, at the very least, confuse you or make you question yourself. Take a minute to count to ten, take a deep breath, or step away. Most importantly, keep your focus on the fact that it *will* be okay. Mishap or no mishap, this recipe will not break you and tomorrow will be another day and another dish.

Celebrate your success

No matter whether this dish turns out to be the very best meal you have ever eaten in your life or the least satisfying meal you have created, you still did it, and that is worth celebrating. The final flavor profile is not the most important factor in this process; the process itself is the most important part. So keep in mind: If you have read this chapter, followed the directions, and put forward your best effort, then you have achieved something and we can throw a party to celebrate that!

Your Recipe

For this one, you are choosing the recipe! You are in charge of your own decisions, preferences, and choices. You can:

- select a recipe from a magazine, online, or a favorite cookbook
- select a recipe from Part 3 of this book
- even go recipe-less and wing it if you'd like.

Remember, too:

- You should select something that appeals to your senses.
- Consider who you will be sharing the dish with and keep them in mind while selecting and cooking.

After you have selected your recipe, think about the tools and ingredients you need to complete the dish. Make sure you have these items ready and available to help ease the process. You can write down the materials and ingredients you will be using here:

Materials

....

....

....

....

Ingredients

Goal Setting

What intention do you have for this session?

....

....

....

....

Name three of your favorite meals:

1. ....

2. ....

3. ....

Name three of your favorite desserts:

1. ....

2. ....

3. ....

Name three of your favorite people:

1. ....

2. ....

3. ....

Time to cook!

1. How did you select your recipe?

....

....

....

....

....

2. Did you select a skill first or did you let the recipe you picked guide you in selecting a skill?

....

....

....

....

....

3. How did you feel about your final dish? Did it meet your expectations?

....

....

....

....

4. What lessons did you learn from this week's cooking assignment?

....

....

....

....

Opportunities for the Future

Keep in mind that I am asking you to identify areas of skill and opportunity in this recipe. The more you practice this ability in the kitchen, the more you should notice yourself being able to do the same outside of the kitchen. When you are assigned a new project at work, what opportunities can you find in that project? Identify the skills you need and how you can tackle the project using these skills. Be aware of what might be more challenging, and work on those challenges as they arise.

Reflection

Use this space to take notes on any ah-ha moments, things you'd like to remember later, things that may have surprised you, moments of clarity during this session, or any questions you have.

Part 3
Get Your Life Back

Chapter 11

After Eight Weeks of Cooking, Now What?

Congratulations! You have completed eight weeks of cooking and practicing the life skills that will lessen your anxiety and lead you to feeling more confident and happy. I hope by this point you are already feeling a difference in your anxiety level. All the work and dedication that you have put in over these last eight weeks will help keep your anxiety at bay. You have made tremendous effort to improve your skills so that when you do feel anxious, you now possess a whole kitchen toolbox of skills to help yourself with, not to mention a few delicious dishes to add to your repertoire.

Remember, though, this is a lifelong process, and you will need to keep your skills sharp and ready for when you need them. I am guessing that right about now you are wondering just how you will do that. This chapter will provide you with a check-in point, a second opportunity to use a diagnostic tool to review your anxiety level after completing eight weeks of cooking and skill building. I will ask you to review your results from the first quiz and this second one and compare the changes. Ideally, your second score will be significantly lower than your first. The reason for the decrease in your score will be a direct result of the tools you have learned and the skills you have been practicing over these last few months.

But if your score didn't change much or maybe even went up, don't give up just yet. Sometimes, we can feel panic when we try something new, and all that means is you need to keep trying and build the new muscles that you have just learned how to work out. Everyone is different: For some people one workout makes a difference, and for others it takes time and repetition to get the desired response. These lessons can be repeated as many times as you need them. With each experience you will become more familiar with the tools, more at ease, and better able to make progress. Just keep in mind the importance of patience and being kind to yourself throughout this journey. The eight weeks is merely just the beginning. This was your first go around learning and being introduced to this new way of managing anxiety.

If your second score was lower than your first, you will find your next step here in Part 3. Please always feel free to revisit any chapter of Part 2 if you need to and even recook the recipe! Those recipes and exercises are there for you to utilize whenever you feel the need. I hope the pages will get smudged with delicious ingredients and worn thin with love.

In order for you to identify where exactly you stand in the process, let's take a minute to reassess your anxiety. Take a deep, calming breath and keep in mind the last few months when answering the following questions. Try to simply focus on each individual question so that you do not get overwhelmed by the evaluation process. Remember, the score itself is not what is most important; rather, it is how you feel and what impact you see and experience in your day-to-day life.

Test Time

This diagnostic tool will help you become more aware of your unique ways of experiencing anxiety and help you to identify your level of anxiety. This check-in will serve as your baseline and help you monitor your feelings and symptoms as you experience and track your progress through the eight-week program in Part 2. Your responses should be based on your general experiences over the last few weeks.

Select the response that best describes the extent to which you experience each symptom.

0 = Not at all 1 = Mild 2 = Moderate 3 = Severe 4 = Very severe

Anxious mood

Worried, waiting for something bad, fearful anticipation, dread

0   1   2   3   4

Tension

Startle easily, restless, unable to relax

0   1   2   3   4

Insomnia

Hard time falling asleep and/or staying asleep, general fatigue, nightmares, lack of motivation

0   1   2   3   4

Depressed mood

Loss of interest, lack of pleasure, sadness, irritability

0   1   2   3   4

Pain

Aches, stiffness, grinding or clenching of the teeth, headaches

0   1   2   3   4

Panic

Palpitations, chest pain or tightness, fainting feeling, hard to breathe

0   1   2   3   4

Fears

Afraid of darkness, strangers, being left alone, being in crowds

0   1   2   3   4

Scoring: Count up the total number of points.

Score total: _____

A total less than 7 means mild anxiety symptoms, 9–12 is mild to moderate, 13–15 is moderate to severe. 16 or above is very severe.

Now that you have completed the second self-assessment, take a moment to think about whether you feel your score matches up with your feelings and observations that you have made throughout the eight weeks of cooking and skill building. Are they in alignment? Does your score reflect the progress that you feel that you have made? Ultimately, a score is merely a number and the feelings that you have are what matter most.

At this stage in the process of exploration, take some time to reflect on the skills and lessons that you have learned. This will allow you the opportunity to articulate just what you have learned and be able to make the connection for yourself moving from recipe to reality.

Let's discuss the real-life situations that commonly occur for so many and think about how we can put these newly honed skills to the test. In this next section, you will find multiple scenarios to think about and consider how your new skills can help ease anxiety when coping with real-life challenging moments outside of the kitchen.

Real-Life Challenge 1

It's Friday afternoon and you just got home from work. All week you have been looking forward to the weekend and relaxing with your partner. You have come up with a few fun ideas for plans to

unwind and enjoy yourselves. Shortly after you arrive home, your partner comes home and they seem upset. They do not seem like themselves. They slam their bag down by the door, toss their shoes off, and stomp upstairs to the other room. You begin to feel your heart beat faster, you swallow hard, and your thoughts race as you wonder what could have happened and what will come next.

What skills do you utilize and how do you put them to use at this moment?

Mindfulness

Stress and time management

Communication

Relationships

Problem solving

Self-esteem

Now that you have taken a moment to identify which skills are needed, think about the way in which you now possess the tools to be able to use these skills. Think for a few minutes about how you would like to respond to this situation. Create your action plan for this moment using concrete examples that put your tools into action.

Action plan:

....

....

....

....

....

....

....

....

....

....

....

Try this:

Take a deep breath, and remember to focus on the here and now. Remember those skills about being present in the moment and not going too far down any rabbit holes just yet. It seems as though there is an opportunity for communication. How are you most comfortable? Do you follow your partner up the stairs and ask them, "What's wrong?" Could you send them a text message and say, "I can tell something must be bothering you. I'm concerned. Can we talk?" Identify your most comfortable way to communicate and give it a try.

Real-Life Challenge 2

You recently got laid off from your job. You had been working at this organization for well over a decade, and after the company was sold and everyone was told that downsizing was coming, you were still blindsided when you were one of the employees to be let go. You thought you had seniority and enough professional respect that you would be spared. No one else from your group of friends has been let go, and you are struggling to have a support system to empathize with you. You are feeling forgotten and devalued and not really sure what next professional steps to take. You just know that this doesn't feel good and you want to feel better—more like yourself and able to make a difference for others.

What skills do you utilize and how do you put them to use at this moment?

Mindfulness

Communication

Problem solving

Stress and time management

Relationships

Self-esteem

Now that you have taken a moment to identify which skills are needed, think about the way in which you now possess the tools to be able to use these skills. Think for a few minutes about how you would like to respond to this situation. Create your action plan for this moment using concrete examples that put your tools into action.

Action plan:

....

....

....

....

....

....

....

....

....

....

Try this:

When we are feeling low, it is so important to find ways for self-expression. Share your feelings and thoughts and what you need.

Find a medium through which you feel most able to express yourself. Think about how you can do something for others. Often, it can help to get out of our head and think about something or someone else.

Real-Life Challenge 3

You are a busy parent, spouse, professional, and many other roles. You constantly feel the tug between your family, your career, and all the other things in life that you are called to, like hobbies and family chores. This specific week you have a large work project that is due and a team of colleagues that are counting on you for your contribution to this project. Your kids have a play at school and a soccer game and there are parent–teacher conferences you must attend. The laundry is piling up, and the dog is in desperate need of a good long walk. Where to even begin?!

What skills do you utilize and how do you put them to use at this moment?

Mindfulness

Stress and time management

Communication

Relationships

Problem solving

Self-esteem

Now that you have taken a moment to identify which skills are needed, think about the way in which you now possess the tools to be able to use these skills. Think for a few minutes about how you would like to respond to this situation. Create your action plan for this moment using concrete examples that put your tools into action.

Action plan:

....

....

....

....

....

....

....

....

....

....

....

Try this:

Consider what *should*s may be weighing on you and your decision-making list. What plan of attack can you attempt when considering how you want to juggle the many to-dos of this busy week? Think about what your priorities are and how you can make decisions that are in line with those priorities. Don't forget to ask for help when you need it and remember that you are not perfect, so do not expect yourself to be.

Real-Life Challenge 4

John is your neighbor who lives down the street. You and John often help each other out when it comes to picking up the mail when someone is out of town, or helping with yard work and other household chores that need multiple sets of hands. John has asked you to help him out this weekend with some minor home renovation projects, and you happily told him you would be able to assist before you remembered you had already made weekend plans.

What skills do you utilize and how do you put them to use at this moment?

Mindfulness

Communication

Problem solving

Stress and time management

Relationships

Self-esteem

Now that you have taken a moment to identify which skills are needed, think about the way in which you now possess the tools to be able to use these skills. Think for a few minutes about how you would like to respond to this situation. Create your action plan for this moment using concrete examples that put your tools into action.

Action plan:

....

....

....

....

....

....

....

....

....

....

....

Try this:

Keep in mind that it is important to identify the problem and determine what goal you have in mind that is best for you. Be sure to brainstorm some ideas and weigh out the pros and cons of those ideas. Once you identify your solution, consider ways in which you can best share and communicate them.

Takeaway time

How do you feel you managed your feelings, reactions, and responses in the real-life challenge section? Did you struggle with anxious thoughts in the same way that you would have eight weeks ago? What was different for you? Were you able to see any themes or commonalities in the areas that you still see yourself struggling with? Those are the areas where I suggest you keep practicing your skills. Be patient: With time, you will continue to feel a decline in anxiety and an increase in abilities that will allow you to live more freely and happily.

Here is a brief summary of each of the focus areas that have been the cornerstone of our work together.

Food and memory

We learned in Chapter 3 that the foundation for all our feelings and frames of reference in life comes from our early memories. Food is a powerful way for us to connect to these memories and to be able to get in touch with the feelings and thoughts that surround specific memories. The sensory experience of food can help transport you back to certain moments in time that you may benefit from some clarity or awareness around these feelings. When something is troubling you, or you see a certain pattern, it can be helpful to ask yourself: "Where did this belief come from?" Exploring the basis for any belief or feeling is a great starting point to try to understand something and recognize if change needs to be made.

Mindfulness

Mindfulness, or the ability to be present in a specific moment in time, is a great gift. Mindfulness can look different for different people. It can take the form of meditation or sitting quietly with your thoughts, or it can happen while acting intentionally to put aside the daily to-do list and choose to pay attention to a specific, finite period of time. You can practice mindfulness on your own or with someone else present whom you are engaged with. This is a skill that needs to be practiced over time with an abundance of patience and effort.

Communication

After learning about the most common styles of communication (see Chapter 5), it is a good idea to reflect and see whether you see your own style present in any of the four common styles. When are you using each style and how is it working for you?

It is noteworthy to keep in mind that communication is about more than our spoken words; it is also about our volume and tone of voice, posture, body language, and eye contact. People pick up on many cues that we send them other than verbal ones.

You also read and learned about the *whys* of communication. Remembering the value in sharing that *why* with someone that we are in contact with can help provide context, deeper understanding, and the ability to remain engaged with someone who matters to us.

Problem solving

Problems and the opportunities to solve those problems exist all around us on any given day. Instead of allowing those problems to fester and grow into insurmountable anxiety, you now have tools to be able to define the problem, determine what your specific goal may be for that problem, brainstorm solutions, weigh out the pros and cons, and be able to identify a realistic, attainable solution to your problem. Being able to see a solution along with a problem is a gift that will continue to serve you as you move through life and come into contact with all types of obstacles. When you can see a problem as a challenge instead of a blockade, it becomes manageable instead of paralyzing.

Stress and time management

If you are someone with a job, with a family, with obligations—in other words if you are human—you are someone that will encounter stress and struggles with time management. Instead of succumbing to these struggles, now you are able to focus on setting the *shoulds* aside, creating a plan for yourself, prioritizing your time and efforts, and deciding on what manageable steps you can take to organize your life. Part of that organization may include asking for help when needed and avoiding the expectation that you or anyone else can do everything all the time. You now know to avoid perfectionist behavior, and unrealistic expectations both of yourself and of those around you.

Relationships

Connection with others is paramount when working to lower anxiety and create moments of happiness. To build these connections, you can now see the importance of being open-minded, and being able to express vulnerability yourself and accept that vulnerability from someone else. Creating that safe space and opportunity for this connection can lead to deeply satisfying attachment and contentment.

Self-esteem

Once you are able to utilize these many skills, you leave room to be able to express yourself creatively and invest in what matters most not only to you but to the other important people around you. Being able to feel a sense of satisfaction, pride, and fulfillment from the use of the tools will allow you to keep anxiety low and joy high. The recipe to this combination now lies within you, and you have the ability to open the pages and select what you need and take the reins for yourself.

What's next?

The next and final chapter of the book will provide you with my call to action to help keep you working on these skills. The chapter offers you 12 additional recipes to cook and practice working on the tasks that can help you to feel better, calmer, less anxious, and happier.

I'd like to take an opportunity to thank you for trying something new and trusting me to help you on your journey to lower anxiety and move toward living a happier life. My hope for you is that this book has made you feel more empowered and confident to keep moving forward in your life and wellness journey. With this book, you have a toolbox full of recipes and skills to help you lessen your anxiety and experience more moments of calm and joy. I hope you will pull this book off the shelf often and read it, cook from it, and find the most meaningful experiences from it. It has been my pleasure being your cooking guide along the way. I wish you lots of sweetness, deliciousness, and, most of all, happiness.

Chapter 12

More Recipes to Maintain Your Skills

This last chapter will provide you with further opportunities to cook, practice, and hone your skills, as well as add some tasty dishes to your cooking repertoire. You will find two additional recipes for each skill (12 new recipes in total) that will help to inspire you to continue your culinary therapy journey. The process will not be as detailed as in Part 2, unless you choose to apply the same process; that is up to you. These recipes will provide a good occasion for you to keep practicing your skills. You should feel free to use these recipes over and over again. The more you revisit them, the more you will find tasks that become meaningful to you in different ways. It's a chance for you to discover actions that help make a difference for you in your life. Each one of us is different, so different aspects will be meaningful in different ways. Because we all experience anxiety differently, we will also experience different actions that can help us to manage our symptoms and struggles.

Although each recipe is listed and connected to a specific theme, keep in mind that you may discover that a recipe may be useful for you in a different way with a different theme. For me, I may find that the process of making soup is an opportunity to practice mindfulness, but for you it may be a great time to work on communication skills or strengthen a relationship with someone specific in your life. I hope you will welcome those opportunities and differences. Each recipe holds a chance for each individual to gain something different and unique.

Like traditional therapy, there comes a time for "maintenance" work. This is the time to utilize periodic check-ins for ongoing upkeep and feeding those ongoing skills that will require lifelong effort and practice. Maintenance work differs depending on the person. You may find that you would like to schedule your maintenance sessions or just know that you are able to pick the book back up anytime you need to. These recipes offer you the chance to stay engaged in your ongoing wellness journey at your own pace.

Here are the recipes that you will find in this chapter.

Mindfulness recipes

East–West Chicken Soup   Dolma (Stuffed Grape Leaves)

Communication recipes

Personal Pizzas   Honey Cake Trifle

Problem-solving recipes

Roasted Vegetable Soup   Cabbage Apple Lime Slaw

Stress and time management recipes

Date and Silan Granola   Assorted Devilish Eggs

Relationship recipes

Roasted Salmon Bowls   Lemon Blueberry Bars

Self-esteem recipes

Candied Kale Salad   Sheet Pan Turmeric Chicken

Mindfulness Recipes

East–West Chicken Soup

I grew up in a Jewish Ashkenazi home where chicken soup as we know it is very common. Boiled chicken parts, a few vegetables, and a little seasoning create this homeopathic cure-all. There's a reason why it's sold in every diner across the country: It's comfort in a bowl. So when I met my Israeli husband almost 20 years ago and he told me he did not eat chicken soup, I was baffled. He is Sephardic: His parents were born in Turkey and Morocco. I don't think they enjoy traditional chicken soup because Sephardic Jews are accustomed to deeper, richer flavors. I was determined to create a chicken soup that everyone would like: A comforting soup that was still a go-to for sick days or when it's freezing cold outside, but also a soup that would include the flavors from my husband's family recipes. East–West soup was born! My family loves it, and it hits the spot, no matter if that spot is North African or European.

Dolma (stuffed vegetables)

Stuffed vegetables of all kinds are comforting, delicious, and so beautiful. Bell peppers are the most typically stuffed vegetable in the United States, but why stop there? The word dolma, or stuffed vegetable, is originally a Turkish word, but this dish is made all over the Middle East and every culture puts its own spin on the flavors.

When my kids were little we had a babysitter who was originally from Iraq. She made the most amazing dolma—stuffed grape leaves, onions (my favorite), zucchini, and baby eggplants. After years of eating her amazing creations, she shared with me how she made them and I put my own spin on them. There are several steps involved, and if you are making a large pot of these amazing treats, be prepared to spend some time in the kitchen.

Why mindfulness?

Both the chicken soup recipe and the dolma recipe will require you to be present in the moment of the experience. The soup takes time, and while it cooks you can use all your senses to ground yourself in the moment. After chopping and mixing, there are wonderful smells and flavors at work. There are several steps to making the dolma, really requiring your full attention in the present moment. Your patience may be tested in the prepping, stuffing, rolling, and cooking, but the payoff is so worthwhile.

East–West Chicken Soup

Ingredients

8–10 generous servings

3 skinless boneless chicken breasts
2 tbsp olive oil
1 large onion, chopped
3 carrots, peeled and chopped
3 celery stalks, chopped
1 leek, washed well and chopped
1 sweet potato, peeled and chopped

1 Yukon Gold potato, peeled and chopped
2 tsp ground turmeric
1 tbsp chicken soup base flavoring
2 tsp kosher salt
1 tsp pepper
Handful of fresh parsley and dill
8 cups water or stock
Cooking twine

Directions

1. In a large stockpot, heat the olive oil over medium heat. Add the chicken breasts and fry for 1–2 minutes until they get slightly golden brown. Flip the chicken and cook on the other side.
2. Add in onions, carrots, celery, leeks, potatoes, turmeric, soup base, and salt and pepper. Mix well until everything is golden and coated with the turmeric.
3. Using the twine, tie the handful of fresh herbs and place on top. Pour the water or stock into the pot. Cover with a lid and bring soup to a boil. Cook over medium heat for about an hour. Taste the soup and adjust the salt and pepper to your taste.
4. Remove the chicken from the soup. Using two forks, shred the chicken on a plate and then add back to the soup. Continue to cook for another 15 minutes. Most of the potato should have melted into the soup and thickened it. Serve hot.

Dolma

Ingredients

8 servings approximately

2 large onions, peeled and sliced down the middle on one side only
1 large tomato
3 zucchini, cut in half
Olive oil
24 grape leaves from a jar

Meat mixture
1½ lb. ground beef
1½ cups basmati rice
1 tbsp Bharat
1 tbsp chicken soup flavoring

½ tsp citric acid
1 tsp kosher salt
½ tsp pepper
1 small can tomato paste
4 cloves garlic

Liquid on top
Juice of 2 large lemons
2 tbsp tamarind concentrate
1 tbsp sugar
2 tbsp pomegranate molasses
1½ cups water

Directions

1. Start by filling a medium pot with water. Bring to a boil and add in the onions. Cook for about 5–10 minutes until the onions soften. Remove the onions from the water. Discard the water. Allow onions to cool until you can separate the layers. Cut the zucchini in half, and use an apple corer to scoop out the flesh from the inside. Cut the top off of a tomato and scoop out the flesh. Lay out a handful of grape leaves.

2. Combine all the ingredients for the meat mixture and then use a spoon to fill all the vegetables. Place about 1–2 teaspoons of meat in the center of a grape leaf, and then

start by rolling the bottom up, then the sides in, and roll up tightly. Fill until all the meat has been used.

3. Use the same pot you boiled the onions in. Drizzle some olive oil on the bottom of the pot. Place the tomato in the center of the pot, add the zucchini around the tomato. Fill in with the onions then the rolled grape leaves on the top. Be sure to pack everything in tightly, leaving no space between the vegetables. Place a small glass plate on top of the vegetables and press down firmly. This will help keep everything in place and prevent some of the meat from spilling out. Once all the ingredients for the liquid are combined, pour over the plate and vegetables. The liquid should just cover the vegetables.

4. Turn the heat to medium high and bring the pot to a boil. Once boiling, lower the heat to medium and cook, covered, for about 30 minutes. Then turn down the heat as low as it will go and simmer for another 60 minutes. Remove the pot from the heat and allow it to sit for about 20 minutes before removing the vegetables from the pot. Serve hot and enjoy!

Communication Recipes

Personal Pizzas

Pizza is a favorite food for so many people. One of the many reasons why I love pizza is because it reminds me of being a little kid in my mom's kitchen. I remember making my own pizza, along with my sister, and then sitting perched in front of the glass oven door watching and waiting for the pizza to be ready and getting to enjoy it with my family. Now clearly you can get a delivery of delicious pizzas from a plethora of pizza stores all over the country, but making your own is so much more satisfying, healthy, economical, and fun.

Honey Cake Trifle

Honey cake is the Jewish version of fruit cake around the New Year holiday. Every family has its own recipe and ways that they eat it. It is a very traditional, old-fashioned cake, but it just so happens that my mom makes a honey cake that really is delicious. My family look forward to it all year long, and when the holiday comes around, my mom is expected to make her honey cake treat. Creative cook that I am, I came up with a fun way to make honey cake feel more updated and modern. Trifle is a really simple, fun way to dress up any dessert. There are so many ingredient options and ways to layer the elements. Plus, it looks beautiful!

Why communication?

Because pizza and trifle both have many options in the way they are made, there is always something to discuss and decide on when preparing them. Are you going to make them as individual treats or larger items for a group? What toppings or additions will be included in the dish? Options mean opportunity for discussion and collaboration. These are great ways to work on communication skills and styles while you are engaged in the process.

Pizza

Ingredients

4–6 personal pizzas or 2 large pizzas

Dough
2 tsp dried yeast
1 tbsp sugar
1½ cups warm water
4 cups flour
2 tbsp olive oil
2 tsp salt

Toppings
Pizza sauce
Shredded cheese

Onions
Mushrooms
Olives
Peppers
Fresh basil
Pepperoni slices
Dry spices like garlic, red pepper flakes, oregano, sea salt... everything but bagel seasoning!
Olive oil (for brushing)

Directions

1. In the bowl of a stand mixer or a large mixing bowl, combine the yeast, sugar, and warm water. Make sure the water isn't hot to the touch, no warmer than 100 °F. Use a fork to mix and then let the mixture proof until the yeast looks frothy and bubbles, about 3–5 minutes. Add the flour, oil, and salt, and mix well until a bowl of dough forms. Knead for a few minutes until the dough is smooth and not very sticky. Allow the dough to rest for at least 10 minutes or up to 2 hours covered with a clean towel or plastic wrap. (Dough can also be stored in the fridge overnight.)

2. Once the dough has rested, use a knife to divide the dough into 4–6 individual portions, or 2 large pizzas.

3. Preheat the oven to 425 °F.

4. One at a time, roll each piece of dough into a circle. Transfer the dough to a pan lined with parchment paper. Spread the sauce, and add any desired toppings. Sprinkle with the seasoning of your choice.

5. Bake for about 15 minutes until the crust has browned slightly and the cheese is bubbling. Enjoy!

Honey Cake Trifle

Ingredients
6 individual glasses or 1 large trifle bowl

Honey cake
¾ cup honey
¾ cup sugar
1 egg
½ tsp baking soda
1 tsp baking powder
¼ cup + 2 tbsp vegetable oil
1 tsp allspice
¼ cup peach schnapps or apricot brandy
1 tbsp cola
¼ tsp salt
½ cup coffee
1¾ cups flour

Apples
2 Honeycrisp apples, peeled and chopped
2 tbsp brown sugar
1 tbsp butter
2 cups whipped cream
1 tsp vanilla extract
Cinnamon for garnish

Directions

1. Preheat the oven to 350 °F.
2. Mix all the ingredients together in a large mixing bowl until combined. Grease an 8 × 8-in. baking pan with nonstick spray and pour batter in the dish. Bake cake for about 35–40 minutes, or until a toothpick comes out clean. Allow the cake to cool for at least 30 minutes before slicing.
3. While the cake is cooling, peel and chop apples. Sauté in a medium pan with brown sugar, butter, and vanilla extract until tender. Set aside.
4. Using individual glass jars or one large bowl assemble the trifle one layer at a time. Place a layer of cake, top it with some apples, and then whipped cream. Repeat another layer. Top the trifle with a sprinkle of cinnamon and serve.

Problem-Solving Recipes

Roasted Vegetable Soup

Winters in Michigan require warm, comforting dishes that help you get through the long, cold, damp months. I love a hot mug or bowl filled with something nourishing I created this roasted vegetable soup during a recent winter when I opened my crisper to see what vegetables I had that could be roasted up and included in a soup. The best part of this dish is that there is no need to panic if you are missing one or more of the ingredients listed. The soup can be made, and will be just as delicious, with many combinations of ingredients. So if you don't have leeks but you have onions—white or red—no problem.

Cabbage Apple Lime Slaw

Coleslaw is a pretty common side dish. It has a way of showing up and being served in many places alongside many different dishes. And sometimes a traditional dish served in a traditional way can be great. Sometimes, however, changing things up a bit can be a really exciting twist. Have you ever had a slaw with jicama or pomegranate seeds? It's worth trying to see if it's something you enjoy as much as I do. The tang from the lime and the sweetness from the honey make a great balance of flavors that work so well together.

Why problem solving?

Vegetables like leeks or jicama are not common ingredients that most people—including me—have on hand on an average day. They are special items that are wonderful to cook with and bring so much flavor to any dish. You need to plan in advance when you want to make these recipes. Sometimes, though, you think of a recipe and want to make it, but you do not have all the required items on hand. One option could be to head over to the grocery store and shop for the ingredients, or you could problem solve! What other similar ingredients do you already have in your crisper or pantry that could be substituted instead of going out and buying the exact items? Is there another way to accomplish a task like making a recipe that works for you? Both these recipes have other possible alternatives; you just need to brainstorm a bit and find a solution.

Roasted Vegetable Soup

Ingredients

8 servings

2 carrots, peeled and chopped
2 leeks, washed and chopped
1 sweet potato, peeled and chopped
2 parsnips, chopped
1 large tomato, halved

2 tbsp olive oil
1 tbsp kosher salt
½ tsp black pepper
1 tsp dried parsley
4 cups vegetable stock or water
⅓ cup heavy cream (optional)

Directions

1. Preheat the oven to 425 °F. Line two baking sheets with parchment paper. Spread chopped veggies on the trays and toss with olive oil, parsley, salt, and pepper. Roast veggies for about 20 minutes until tender and slightly browned.

2. Remove the roasted vegetables from the oven, add them to a large pot, then pour over the stock or water.

3. Bring to a boil and then turn off heat. Use an immersion blender (or regular blender) to mix soup until creamy and smooth. If liked, add a swirl of cream on top to make the soup richer. Serve hot.

Cabbage Apple Lime Slaw

Ingredients

Serves about 16 people

1 head of green cabbage, thinly sliced
2 Granny Smith apples, cut into matchsticks (no need to peel)
1 jicama, peeled and cut into matchsticks
¼ cup pomegranate seeds

Dressing
2 tbsp apple cider vinegar
1 lime, zest and juice
¼ tbsp apple cider (or juice)
2 tbsp Dijon mustard
1 tbsp poppy seeds
1 tbsp kosher salt
2 tsp sugar
¼ cup vegetable oil

Directions

1. In a large mixing bowl, combine the four ingredients for the slaw.

2. Then in a jar with a lid, combine all the ingredients for the dressing. Shake well until all combined and slightly thickened. Adjust the taste to make it sweeter or saltier to your liking.

3. Dress the salad up to an hour in advance of serving to allow the cabbage to soften slightly but remain crunchy. Serve room temperature or cold.

Stress and Time Management Recipes

Date and Silan Granola

Granola can be easily purchased in many stores. I have bought lots of different brands and flavors over the years. It's a great item to keep in your pantry to pull out and add some crunch and some nutrients to salads, yogurt, and smoothies. Usually, though, I find they all taste the same. And oftentimes there are many other ingredients listed on the bag that I struggle to pronounce. The price tag is often pretty high as well.

So at some point, I decided I was done with the mediocre store-bought versions and was going to try making my own. I went to the pantry and combined different ingredients that I had and found some ways to flavor a batch that was a little different and unique. It came out delicious and was such a simple way to create something that felt so special.

Assorted Devilish Eggs

Eggs are one of my favorite foods. They're my go-to protein most days and the ways you can use eggs are endless. I love eggs in every shape and form. Deviled eggs are the best combo of creamy and tangy and a great crowd pleaser to serve up to others. But you know me: I love changing things up and bringing my own flare to every dish, hence my Devilish Eggs. They are a great way to add lots of different flavor combinations to something traditional, and they are oh so loved.

Why stress and time management?

These two seemingly simple dishes don't appear at first glance to be anything complicated or difficult. But they both have a hidden trick to them. The timing needs to be just right for both. Neither of these dishes is a "set it and forget it"-type recipe. They both require a very specific amount of time, otherwise you risk burning or overcooking the dish. If you do follow things just so, they can be very simple recipes, but if you do not, you may find yourself in that panic moment of needing to either start over or be prepared to be very disappointed by the outcome.

Date and Silan Granola

Ingredients

Yields 1 large jar

2¼ cups oats
½ cup pecans or almonds
¼ cup sunflower seeds
¼ cup dried dates
¼ cup coconut flakes
½ tsp sea salt

½ tsp cinnamon
⅛ tsp cardamom
1 tbsp vanilla
3 tbsp olive oil
¼ cup Silan or honey

Directions

1. Preheat the oven to 375 °F.

2. Combine all the ingredients in a large mixing bowl. Toss well so that all the ingredients are coated thoroughly with the oil and Silan/honey.

3. Line a baking sheet with parchment paper and pour the mixture into a single layer. Use a spatula to spread the mixture out evenly.

4. Bake for about 12–15 minutes until golden. Be careful not to burn. Even if it looks underdone, it will harden as it cools. Store in an airtight jar for up to 2 weeks.

5. Serve the granola over a cup of Greek yogurt and fresh fruit.

Assorted Devilish Eggs

Ingredients

20 egg halves

10 eggs
2 soft avocados
1 tomato
1 shallot, diced
2 jalapeno peppers, 1 diced, seeds removed (optional), and 1 sliced thinly for garnish

1 lime, zest and juice
½ tsp salt
½ tsp pepper
½ tsp (or more) hot sauce
2 tbsp mayo

Directions

1. Place the uncooked eggs in a medium pot with 1 tablespoon salt and fill until covered with cold water. Turn the heat on high and bring to a boil. Once the water is boiling, cover the pot and turn the heat to low and cook for 5–6 minutes to get perfectly jammy eggs.
2. Once cooked, turn off the heat and place the eggs in a bowl of ice and cold water. Allow them to cool completely before peeling.
3. Peel the eggs and cut them in half, scoop out the yolks and place them in a mixing bowl. Scoop out the avocado and add to the yolks, and the chopped tomato, onion, pepper, hot sauce, mayo, lime zest, lime juice, salt, and pepper. Smash with the back of a fork and mix all together until well combined. Add more salt and pepper to your taste. Then scoop a spoonful back into each of the egg halves. Garnish with a jalapeno slice. Serve and enjoy!

Relationship Recipes

Roasted Salmon Bowls

Roasted salmon bowls are made weekly in my house. This meal is such a great quick, simple, and healthy dinner that can be enjoyed in so many different ways. This is by far my daughter's favorite dish, and I am always happy to make her salmon because I love it, too. This is a perfect complete meal with all the food groups and all the flavor profiles. The textures and colors are so balanced and beautiful; it makes me feel good just looking at this dish filled with gorgeous foods.

Lemon Blueberry Bars

The combination of lemon and blueberry is one of my favorites. There is something about the mix of colors and the mix of flavors that makes for the most perfect pairing. Tart lemon and sweet berry flavors make the best balance. The day I made this recipe for the first time, I got a call from my very best friend telling me she had become an aunt, to a beautiful baby girl named Stevie. From that day on, we call these bars "Stevie bars." It was a wonderful memory that was created in the sweetest of ways.

Why relationships?

Dinnertime is a time for connection, and when that can be done over a meal that everyone is happy about, the connection is so much easier. When you have the ability to create your own version of something, there is no need to argue or pick and choose. You can do it your own way at the same time as doing something together. Baking a treat and sharing that treat with someone you love offers connections which enhance relationships. Both these recipes are great opportunities to enhance these skills and find ways to keep working on that ability to connect with those you care about.

Roasted Salmon Bowls

Ingredients

Serves 4

4 salmon filets (6–7 oz per piece)
1 tsp avocado oil
½ tsp granulated garlic
½ tsp kosher salt
½ tsp pepper
½ tsp onion powder
½ tsp paprika
½ tsp grated lime zest
½ tsp honey
1 tbsp soy sauce
1½ cups dry sushi rice

¼ tsp salt
2 cups water

Suggested toppings for your bowl
Seaweed
Edamame
Crab sticks
Shredded cabbage
Cucumber or carrot sticks
Mango
Sriracha/soy/mayo

Directions

1. Preheat the oven to 425 °F.
2. Line a sheet pan with parchment paper, pat dry the salmon filets with paper towel. Drizzle them with the oil, and then sprinkle with seasoning, honey, and soy sauce.
3. Roast for about 10–15 minutes, or until they are cooked how you like them.
4. Add the rice to a small pot. Add salt and water and mix well. Bring the rice to a rolling boil, then reduce heat to low and cover the pot with its lid. Allow to cook for about 15 minutes without removing the lid. Once the rice has absorbed all the water, fluff up with a fork and serve.
5. Add cooked rice to a bowl, and top with flaked pieces of salmon plus any desired toppings. Discuss with your partner which toppings you selected and why.

Lemon Blueberry Bars

Ingredients

Yields about two dozen pieces

2½ cups flour
2 tsp baking powder
¼ tsp salt
1 cup sugar
¾ cup vegetable oil

3 eggs
1 tsp vanilla extract
1 lemon, zest and juice
½ cup dried blueberries
Turbinado sugar

Directions

1. Preheat the oven to 350 °F.

2. Mix all the ingredients together in a large bowl until a uniform dough forms.

3. Line a large baking sheet with parchment paper. Divide the dough in half. On the baking sheet, form two long, smooth logs with the dough. Sprinkle logs with Turbinado sugar.

4. Bake for 20 minutes. Remove from the oven and allow the bars to cool for about 20 minutes before slicing them into sticks. Place the bars on their side, sprinkle with more sugar, and return to the oven for another 5 minutes. Turn the oven off and leave the bars in the warm oven for 10–15 minutes.

5. Remove from the oven and allow to cool completely before storing in an airtight container or freezing.

Self-Esteem Recipes

Candied Kale Salad

I am a big fan of salad, and I am a big fan of kale. It's a superfood, but it isn't so super if you do not know how to use it. So often people think they do not like kale because it can be very rough and hard to chew if you do not give it the proper love it requires. Whenever I make this salad, my guests are surprised how delicious it is and how they can actually enjoy kale. Nothing makes me happier than showing people how delicious healthy foods can be used in the best, most scrumptious ways — especially when paired with lots of sweet ingredients that bring perfect balance.

Sheet Pan Turmeric Chicken

We eat lots of chicken. It's a great healthy protein that really is a blank canvas for whatever flavors you like. I have found that this one-pan dinner is great for a quick, easy weeknight meal that packs a lot of flavor punch and is beautiful enough to serve if you want to impress guests. Often, I have found that people can be nervous about cooking with chicken. They are not confident about the preparation or the outcome, so they avoid it. This dish is foolproof because the boneless chicken cooks much faster than bone-in pieces and it can provide a sense of safety to the cook. The lemon and turmeric combo is beautiful, and the fennel is an unexpected flavor that brightens the warm, oven-cooked dish.

Why self-esteem?

When you are preparing "scary" foods like kale and chicken and you can pull them off successfully, you will experience the smiles of joy that come not only to your guests' faces but to yours, too. These are dishes that will make you feel a sense of accomplishment that is imperative to building confidence and fostering self-esteem. When your family or friends come back to you and request these delicious dishes, you will feel more and more confident each time.

Candied Kale Salad with Sweet Balsamic Dressing

Ingredients

Serves 6 approximately

1 bunch of Tuscan kale, rinsed, dried well, stems removed, chopped
1 tsp olive oil
1 large sweet potato, washed and chopped
1 apple, chopped
2 tbsp pomegranate seeds
2 tbsp dried cherries
2 tbsp sunflower seeds
2 tbsp walnuts or pecans, chopped

½ red onion, thinly sliced
Feta or goat cheese crumble (optional)

Dressing
1 tsp Dijon mustard
1 tbsp balsamic vinegar
½ tsp salt
¼ tsp pepper
1 tbsp brown sugar
1 tbsp honey
⅓ cup vegetable oil

Directions

1. Preheat the oven to 400 °F. Place the chopped sweet potato on a baking sheet. Toss with some olive oil and salt. Roast for about 10–15 minutes until tender and slightly browned. Allow to cool.

2. Once your kale is cleaned, stems removed, and chopped, place in a large mixing bowl. Drizzle 1 teaspoon olive oil over the kale and, using your hands, mix well. This process of "massaging" the kale will soften the leaves and take away some of the bitterness. Once all the oil is mixed in, you can top with the other salad ingredients.

3. In a small jar or cup, combine all the ingredients for the dressing. Mix well with a fork or shake well with the lid on tightly. Mix until the oil is fully incorporated into the dressing. Drizzle over the salad and serve.

Sheet Pan Turmeric Chicken

Ingredients

Serves 4 approximately

1 lb. small potatoes
4–5 rainbow carrots, peeled and sliced on a bias
1 large sweet onion, chopped
3 skinless boneless chicken breasts, sliced into thin pieces
1 tsp + ½ tsp ground turmeric
½ tsp + ½ tsp granulated garlic
½ tsp + ½ tsp kosher salt
¼ tsp + ¼ tsp black pepper
½ tsp onion powder
1 tbsp chicken soup bouillon powder
1–2 tsp olive oil
1 lemon, sliced
½ cup fennel, shaved

Directions

1. Preheat the oven to 400 °F.
2. On a large baking pan lined with a piece of parchment paper, lay out the potatoes, onions, and carrots. Drizzle over a half teaspoon of olive oil, plus a half teaspoon each of turmeric, granulated garlic, and salt and a quarter teaspoon of pepper. Toss to coat. Roast for about 15 minutes.
3. While the veggies are roasting, place the raw chicken in a mixing bowl with half teaspoons of turmeric, granulated garlic, salt, and onion powder, plus the quarter teaspoon of pepper and the tablespoon chicken soup bouillon powder. Drizzle 1–2 teaspoons of olive oil and toss to coat. Remove the pan with the veggies from the oven, add the chicken, and carefully mix with the carrots, onions, and potatoes. Arrange the lemon slices over the chicken and scatter over the fennel as well. Place the pan back in the 400 °F oven for another 15–20 minutes, or until the chicken is cooked through. Serve hot. Enjoy!

Acknowledgments

Rachel Landes and the Sheldon team: Thank you for taking a chance on this idea and making my dreams become a book reality. Working with you has been a pleasure and appreciated on every level.

Julia Pastore, my first editor: Thank you for your patience and talent, which led to the next steps in making this book real.

Ellen Yashinsky Chute: Thank you for seeing the potential in that young MSW student. Your unwavering support and mentorship helped shape me into the clinician that I am today. I will always look up to you as my mentor and my friend.

Lucinda Scala Quinn and Adeena Sussman: Your willingness to help someone unknown has touched me more than I can express. It is professionals and kindhearted people like you who help pave the way for other women to leave their mark in this world. Thank you for your time, kindness, and support along the way.

My cheerleading squad of friends: How lucky can one girl be? Thank you to my ride-or-dies—you know who you are! I cannot tell you how much your love, support, and patience are appreciated. My life is so much better with you and your neverending encouragement of my dreams. Thank you to each of you for always being interested in my projects, listening to me and believing in me, even when I had my doubts. I love you all.

My clients: Thank you to my students from many years ago who came to visit and ate candy from my coffee table and trusted me with their high school ups and downs. You all have a place in my heart. You taught me how to be the clinician I wanted to be. To my clients over the years that trusted me with their struggles and feelings, it has been an honor and a privilege to work with you. To those of you who humored me by chopping vegetables in the office, or allowed me into your home kitchens over video, I have learned from each of you and I hope our work has had a positive impact for you.

All the friends and loved ones who have dined with me and my family over the years: You have inspired my cooking and shaped my desire to help others. Thank you for always being gracious and willing to taste, share, and give my family and me the pleasure of your company around our table.

Alisha T. Zucker: You are my constant rock and an incredible friend, my biggest advocate and believer. I wouldn't be where I am today without you. You pushed me forward when I had doubts or when I couldn't see my own potential. You have invested so many hours in our friendship, loving me, helping me, and inspiring me. Thank you for editing, for texting, for calling, for visiting, for tasting, and, most of all, for making this Lulabelle always feel so very loved. I adore you.

Mom, Dad, and Ray: I truly believe that I have the best parents and sister in the world. I feel your love and support each and every day. You guys have always seen me and loved me for exactly the person I am and made me feel special for it. Thank you for boosting me up, for celebrating my wins, and always being proud of me just as I am. It will always be an understatement to tell you that I am grateful. I love each of you so much for loving me exactly the way that I needed.

Ofer: My love, my partner, my best supporter. What you have given me is what has allowed me to achieve everything I have in life. You have truly made each and every one of my dreams come true. Thank you for always supporting my dreams and wishes and encouraging me to do whatever it is that I have needed to do to make my every wish come true. The life that we have built together is perfect in every best and imperfect way. I love you.

My Avitali and Shai: Everything I do is for you. I live for you to be proud of your Ema and to show you both that the road is paved with every possibility you could ever dream of. Nothing has made me happier in life than cooking for you, feeding you, nourishing you, and watching you grow to do the same for others in your own amazing ways. I love you endlessly and I will always be here to feed your bellies and, most importantly, your spirit. Thank you for being mine.

References

Beaumont, Pauline (2020). *Bread Therapy: The Mindful Art of Baking Bread*. Boston, MA: Houghton Mifflin Harcourt.

DeSena, Dan, et al. *Cognitive-Behavioral Therapy (CBT) Group Program for Depression*. University of Michigan Department of Psychiatry.

Colwin, Laurie (2014). *Home Cooking*. New York: Vintage.

Coordinator (2017). "Managing and reducing anxiety." *AdultMentalHealth.org*, March 27, available at adultmentalhealth.org/managing-and-reducing-anxiety/

Ducharme, Jamie (2018). "5 ways love is good for your health." *Time*, February 14, available at time.com/5136409/health-benefits-love/

D'Zurilla, T. J., and Goldfried, M. R. (1971). "Problem solving and behavior modification." *Journal of Abnormal Psychology*, 78(1), 107–26. https://doi.org/10.1037/h0031360

Flinn, Allie (2019). "Therapeutic cooking is meditation for people who love to eat (or hate to sit still)." *Well+Good*, April 18, available at www.wellandgood.com/food/therapeutic-cooking-meditation

Green, Jeffrey D., Reid, Chelsea A., Kneuer, Margaret A., and Hedgebeth, Mattie V. (2023). "The Proust effect: scents, food, and nostalgia." *Current Opinion in Psychology* 50 (April): 101562. https://doi.org/10.1016/j.copsyc.2023.101562

Hebert, Elizabeth A., Dugas, Michel J., Tulloch, Tyler G., and Holowka, Darren W. (2014). "Positive beliefs about worry: A psychometric evaluation of the Why Worry-II." *Personality and Individual Differences*, 56(3). https://doi.org/10.1016/j.paid.2013.08.009

Langer, Stephen M. (2014). *Solution-Focused Brief Therapy: What Is It & What's the Evidence?* Northwest Brief Therapy Training Center.

National Institute of Mental Health (2024). "Any anxiety disorder." *National Institute of Mental Health*, available at www.nimh.nih.gov/health/statistics/any-anxiety-disorder

U.S. Centers for Disease Control and Prevention (2024). "Social connection," available at www.cdc.gov/social-connectedness/about/index.html

Whalen, Jeanne (2014). "A road to mental health through the kitchen." *Wall Street Journal*, December 8, available at www.wsj.com/articles/a-road-to-mental-health-through-the-kitchen-1418059204

Wickramaratne Priya J., et al. (2022). "Social connectedness as a determinant of mental health: A scoping review." *PLoS One* 17(10): e0275004. https://doi.org/10.1371/journal.pone.0275004

Index